To: _____

From: _____

Resources by Lee Strobel

The Case for Christ
The Case for Christ audio
The Case for Christ — Student Edition (with Jane Vogel)
The Case for Christ curriculum (with Garry Poole)
The Case for Christmas
The Case for Christmas audio
The Case for a Creator
The Case for a Creator audio
The Case for a Creator — Student Edition (with Jane Vogel)
The Case for a Creator curriculum (with Garry Poole)
The Case for Easter
The Case for Faith
The Case for Faith audio
The Case for Faith — Student Edition (with Jane Vogel)
The Case for Faith curriculum (with Garry Poole)
The Case for the Real Jesus
The Case for the Real Jesus audio
Discussing the Da Vinci Code curriculum (with Garry Poole)
Discussing the Da Vinci Code discussion guide (with Garry Poole)
Exploring the Da Vinci Code (with Garry Poole)
Experiencing the Passion of Jesus (with Garry Poole)
Faith Under Fire curriculum series
God's Outrageous Claims
Inside the Mind of Unchurched Harry and Mary
Off My Case for Kids
Surviving a Spiritual Mismatch in Marriage (with Leslie Strobel)
Surviving a Spiritual Mismatch in Marriage audio
What Jesus Would Say

Other Resources by Garry Poole

The Complete Book of Questions
Seeker Small Groups
The Three Habits of Highly Contagious Christians

In the Tough Questions Series:

Don't All Religions Lead to God?
How Could God Allow Suffering and Evil?
How Does Anyone Know God Exists?
Why Become a Christian?
Tough Questions Leader's Guide (with Judson Poling)

THE CASE FOR EASTER

A Journalist Investigates the Evidence for the Resurrection

LEE STROBEL

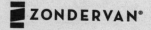 ZONDERVAN®

ZONDERVAN

The Case for Easter
Copyright © 1998, 2003 by Lee Strobel

This is an excerpt from *The Case for Christ* Copyright © 1998

Requests for information should be addressed to:

Zondervan, Grand Rapids, Michigan 49530

This Edition: ISBN 978-0-310-33950-2

Interior design by Sherri L. Hoffman

Printed in the United States of America

16 17 18 /QGM/ 20 19 18 17 16 15 14 13 12 11 10 9 8 7

CONTENTS

INTRODUCTION

I picked up my phone at the *Chicago Tribune* and was assaulted by the sobbing, frantic voice of a distraught father. His nineteen-year-old daughter was missing, he said. She was a good girl, never in any trouble, not much more than an innocent child—and now she was gone. The police weren't helping. Could I alert the city to her disappearance?

Moved by his anguish, I began to pursue the story. But when I interviewed his daughter's friends and the police, a much different story emerged. Tragically, it turned out she had been a drug addict, a petty criminal, the girlfriend of a gang member, and a part-time prostitute. When police found her body a few days later, they determined she had been the victim of a heroin overdose.

I didn't have the heart to tell her father all the details I had learned about her lifestyle. He sincerely believed she was an innocent child, but he had been wrong. His love for his daughter had blinded him. He had seen what he wanted to see, overlooking obvious clues that pointed in another direction. As a parent myself, I could hardly blame him for his wishful thinking.

To me—an atheist at the time—this was an apt analogy for the mindset of Christians. From my perspective, their faith blinded them to the real facts about Jesus, and they only saw what they wanted to see in him. Certainly he was only a legend or a mere mortal at best. In their wide-eyed gullibility, Christians sincerely believed he rose from the dead and thus proved he was the Son of God.

But there was no doubt in my mind that they were sincerely wrong.

They had to be! As a reporter, I had seen lots of dead people—and none of them had ever come back to life. Christians could spin fanciful tales of an empty tomb, but they could never change the grim, absolute finality of death.

Then the unthinkable happened—my wife became a Christian. I anticipated the worst, and yet in the ensuing months I began to see winsome changes in her character and values. When she attributed this transformation to God, I knew it was time to use my journalism and legal training to thoroughly investigate Christianity. Maybe I could liberate her from this cult!

The starting point seemed obvious to me: clearly, the resurrection was the linchpin of the Christian faith. After all, anyone can claim to be the Son of God. But if someone could substantiate that assertion by returning to life after being certifiably dead and buried—well, that would be a compelling confirmation that he was telling the truth. Even for a skeptic like me.

As I began my investigation, three questions loomed: Was Jesus really dead after his ordeal on the cross? Was his tomb actually empty on that first Easter Morning? And did credible people subsequently encounter him? I decided to pursue these issues in order, starting with the medical evidence about the supposed demise of Jesus.

If these questions have ever intrigued you, then join me in the following pages as I retrace and expand upon the journey that unexpectedly ended up shaking my spiritual cynicism to its core.

THE MEDICAL EVIDENCE: WAS JESUS' DEATH A SHAM AND HIS RESURRECTION A HOAX?

I paused to read the plaque hanging in the waiting room of a doctor's office: "Let conversation cease. Let laughter flee. This is the place where death delights to help the living."

Obviously, this was no ordinary physician. I was paying another visit to Dr. Robert J. Stein, one of the world's foremost forensic pathologists, a flamboyant, husky-voiced medical detective who used to regale me with stories about the unexpected clues he had uncovered while examining corpses. For him, dead men *did* tell tales — in fact, tales that would often bring justice to the living.

During his lengthy tenure as medical examiner of Cook County, Illinois, Stein performed thousands of autopsies, each time meticulously searching for insights into the circumstances surrounding the victim's death. Repeatedly his sharp eye for detail, his encyclopedic knowledge of the human anatomy, and his uncanny investigative intuition helped this medical sleuth reconstruct the victim's violent demise.

Sometimes innocent people were vindicated as a result of his findings. But more often Stein's work was the final nail in a defendant's coffin. Such was the case with John

Wayne Gacy, who faced the executioner after Stein helped convict him of thirty-three grisly murders.

That's how crucial medical evidence can be. It can determine whether a child died of abuse or an accidental fall. It can establish whether a person succumbed to natural causes or was murdered by someone who spiked the person's coffee with arsenic. It can uphold or dismantle a defendant's alibi by pinpointing the victim's time of death, using an ingenious procedure that measures the amount of potassium in the eyes of the deceased.

And yes, even in the case of someone brutally executed on a Roman cross two millennia ago, medical evidence can still make a crucial contribution: it can help determine whether the resurrection of Jesus—the supreme vindication of his claim to deity—was nothing more than an elaborate hoax. With Stein having impressed on me the value of forensic clues, I knew it was time to seek out a medical expert who has thoroughly investigated the historical facts concerning the crucifixion and has managed to separate truth from legend.

RESURRECTION OR RESUSCITATION?

The idea that Jesus never really died on the cross can be found in the Koran,[1] which was written in the seventh century—in fact, Ahmadiya Muslims contend that Jesus actually fled to India. To this day there's a shrine that supposedly marks his real burial place in Srinagar, Kashmir.[2]

As the nineteenth century dawned, Karl Bahrdt, Karl Venturini, and others tried to explain away the resurrection by suggesting that Jesus only fainted from exhaustion on the cross, or he had been given a drug that made him appear to die, and that he had later been revived by the cool, damp air of the tomb.[3]

Conspiracy theorists bolstered this hypothesis by pointing out that Jesus had been given some liquid on a sponge while on the cross (Mark 15:36) and that Pilate seemed surprised at how quickly Jesus had succumbed (Mark 15:44). Consequently, they said, Jesus' reappearance wasn't a miraculous resurrection but merely a fortuitous resuscitation, and his tomb was empty because he continued to live.

While reputable scholars have repudiated this so-called swoon theory, it keeps recurring in popular literature. In 1929 D. H. Lawrence wove this theme into a short story in which he suggested that Jesus had fled to Egypt, where he fell in love with the priestess Isis.[4]

In 1965 Hugh Schonfield's best-seller *The Passover Plot* alleged that it was only the unanticipated stabbing of Jesus by the Roman soldier that foiled his complicated scheme to escape the cross alive, even though Schonfield conceded, "We are nowhere claiming ... that [the book] represents what actually happened."[5]

The swoon hypothesis popped up again in Donovan Joyce's 1972 book *The Jesus Scroll*, which "contains an even more incredible string of improbabilities than Schonfield's," according to resurrection expert Gary Habermas.[6] In 1982, *Holy Blood, Holy Grail* added the twist that Pontius Pilate had been bribed to allow Jesus to be taken down from the cross before he was dead. Even so, the authors confessed, "We could not—and still cannot—prove the accuracy of our conclusion."[7]

As recently as 1992, a little-known academic from Australia, Barbara Thiering, caused a stir by reviving the swoon theory. Her book, *Jesus and the Riddle of the Dead Sea Scrolls,* was introduced with much fanfare by a well-respected US publisher and then derisively dismissed by Emory University scholar Luke Timothy Johnson as being "the purest poppycock, the product of fevered imagination rather than careful analysis."[8]

Today, the swoon theory continues to flourish. I hear it all the time. But what does the evidence really establish? What actually happened at the Crucifixion? What was Jesus' cause of death? Is there any possible way he could have survived this ordeal? Those are the kinds of questions that I hoped medical evidence could help resolve.

So I flew to southern California and knocked on the door of a prominent physician who has extensively studied the historical, archaeological, and medical data concerning the death of Jesus of Nazareth — although it seems that, due to the mysteriously missing body, no autopsy has ever been performed.

INTERVIEW WITH ALEXANDER METHERELL, M.D., PH.D.

The plush setting was starkly incongruous with the subject we were discussing. There we were, sitting in the living room of Dr. Metherell's comfortable California home on a balmy spring evening, warm ocean breezes whispering through the windows, while we were talking about a topic of unimaginable brutality: a beating so barbarous that it shocks the conscience, and a form of capital punishment so depraved that it stands as wretched testimony to man's inhumanity to man.

I had sought out Metherell because I heard he possessed the medical and scientific credentials to explain the Crucifixion. But I also had another motivation: I had been told he could discuss the topic dispassionately as well as accurately. That was important to me because I wanted the facts to speak for themselves, without the hyperbole or charged language that might otherwise manipulate emotions.

As you would expect from someone with a medical degree (University of Miami in Florida) and a doctorate in engineering (University of Bristol in England), Metherell speaks with scientific precision. He is board-certified in diagnosis by the American Board of Radiology and has been a consultant to the National Heart, Lung, and Blood Institute of the National Institutes of Health of Bethesda, Maryland.

A former research scientist who has taught at the University of California, Metherell is editor of five scientific books and has written for publications ranging from *Aerospace Medicine* to *Scientific American*. His ingenious analysis of muscular contraction has been published in *The Physiologist* and *Biophysics Journal*. He even looks the role of a distinguished medical authority: he's an imposing figure with silver hair and a courteous yet formal demeanor.

I'll be honest: at times I wondered what was going on inside Dr. Metherell's head. With scientific reserve, speaking slowly and methodically, he gave no hint of any inner turmoil as he calmly described the chilling details of Jesus' demise. Whatever was going on underneath, whatever distress it caused him as a Christian to talk about the cruel fate that befell Jesus, he was able to mask with a professionalism born out of decades of laboratory research.

He just gave me the facts—and after all, that was what I was after.

THE TORTURE BEFORE THE CROSS

Initially, I wanted to elicit from Metherell a basic description of the events leading up to Jesus' death. So after a time of social chat, I put down my iced tea and shifted in my chair to face him squarely. "Could you paint a picture of what happened to Jesus?" I asked.

He cleared his throat. "It began after the Last Supper," he said. "Jesus went with his disciples to the Mount of Olives—specifically, to the Garden of Gethsemane. And there, if you remember, he prayed all night. Now, during that process he was anticipating the coming events of the next day. Since he knew the amount of suffering he was going to have to endure, he was quite naturally experiencing a great deal of psychological stress."

I raised my hand to stop him. "Whoa—here's where skeptics have a field day," I told him. "The gospels tell us he began to sweat blood at this point. Now, c'mon, isn't that just a product of some overactive imaginations? Doesn't that call into question the accuracy of the gospel writers?"

Unfazed, Metherell shook his head. "Not at all," he replied. "This is a known medical condition called *hematidrosis*. It's not very common, but it is associated with a high degree of psychological stress.

"What happens is that severe anxiety causes the release of chemicals that break down the capillaries in the sweat glands. As a result, there's a small amount of bleeding into these glands, and the sweat comes out tinged with blood. We're not talking about a lot of blood; it's just a very, very small amount."

Though a bit chastened, I pressed on. "Did this have any other effect on the body?"

"What this did was set up the skin to be extremely fragile so that when Jesus was flogged by the Roman soldier the next day, his skin would be very, very sensitive."

Well, I thought, here we go. I braced myself for the grim images I knew were about to flood my mind. I had seen plenty of dead bodies as a journalist — casualties of car accidents, fires, and crime syndicate retribution — but there was something especially unnerving in hearing about someone being intentionally brutalized by executioners determined to extract maximum suffering.

"Tell me," I said, "what was the flogging like?"

Metherell's eyes never left me. "Roman floggings were known to be terribly brutal. They usually consisted of thirty-nine lashes but frequently were a lot more than that, depending on the mood of the soldier applying the blows.

"The soldier would use a whip of braided leather thongs with metal balls woven into them. When the whip would strike the flesh, these balls would cause deep bruises or contusions, which would break open with further blows. And the whip had pieces of sharp bone as well, which would cut the flesh severely.

"The back would be so shredded that part of the spine was sometimes exposed by the deep, deep cuts. The whipping would have gone all the way from the shoulders down to the back, the buttocks, and the back of the legs. It was just terrible."

Metherell paused. "Go on," I said.

"One physician who has studied Roman beatings said, 'As the flogging continued, the lacerations would tear into the underlying skeletal muscles and produce quivering ribbons of bleeding flesh.' A third-century historian by the name of Eusebius described a flogging by saying, 'The sufferer's veins were laid bare, and the very muscles, sinews, and bowels of the victim were open to exposure.'

"We know that many people would die from this kind of beating even before they could be crucified. At the least, the victim would experience tremendous pain and go into hypovolemic shock."

Metherell had thrown in a medical term I didn't know. "What does *hypovolemic shock* mean?" I asked.

"*Hypo* means 'low,' *vol* refers to volume, and *emic* means 'blood,' so *hypovolemic shock* means the person is suffering the effects of losing a large amount of blood," the doctor explained. "This does four things. First, the heart races to try to pump blood that isn't there; second, the blood pressure drops, causing fainting or collapse; third, the kidneys stop producing urine to maintain what volume is left; and fourth, the person becomes very thirsty as the body craves fluids to replace the lost blood volume."

"Do you see evidence of this in the gospel accounts?"

"Yes, most definitely," he replied. "Jesus was in hypovolemic shock as he staggered up the road to the execution site at Calvary, carrying the horizontal beam of the cross. Finally Jesus collapsed, and the Roman soldier ordered Simon to carry the cross for him. Later we read that Jesus said, 'I thirst,' at which point a sip of vinegar was offered to him.

"Because of the terrible effects of this beating, there's no question that Jesus was already in serious to critical condition even before the nails were driven through his hands and feet."

THE AGONY OF THE CROSS

As distasteful as the description of the flogging was, I knew that even more repugnant testimony was yet to come. That's because historians are unanimous that Jesus survived the beating that day and went on to the cross—which is where the real issue lies.

These days, when condemned criminals are strapped down and injected with poisons or secured to a wooden chair and subjected to a surge of electricity, the circumstances are highly controlled. Death comes quickly and predictably. Medical examiners carefully certify the victim's passing. From close proximity witnesses scrutinize everything from beginning to end.

But how certain was death by this crude, slow, and rather inexact form of execution called crucifixion? In fact, most people aren't sure how the cross kills its victims. And without a trained medical examiner to officially attest that Jesus had died, might he have escaped the experience brutalized and bleeding but nevertheless alive?

I began to unpack these issues. "What happened when he arrived at the site of the crucifixion?" I asked.

"He would have been laid down, and his hands would have been nailed in the outstretched position to the horizontal beam. This crossbar was called the *patibulum,* and at this stage it was separate from the vertical beam, which was permanently set in the ground."

I was having difficulty visualizing this; I needed more details. "Nailed with what?" I asked. "Nailed where?"

"The Romans used spikes that were five to seven inches long and tapered to a sharp point. They were driven through the wrists," Metherell said, pointing about an inch or so below his left palm.

"Hold it," I interrupted. "I thought the nails pierced his palms. That's what all the paintings show. In fact, it's become a standard symbol representing the crucifixion."

"Through the wrists," Metherell repeated. "This was a solid position that would lock the hand; if the nails had been driven through the palms, his weight would have caused the skin to tear and he would have fallen off the cross. So the nails went through the wrists, although this was considered part of the hand in the language of the day.

"And it's important to understand that the nail would go through the place where the median nerve runs. This is the largest nerve going out to the hand, and it would be crushed by the nail that was being pounded in."

Since I have only a rudimentary knowledge of the human anatomy, I wasn't sure what this meant. "What sort of pain would that have produced?" I asked.

"Let me put it this way," he replied. "Do you know the kind of pain you feel when you bang your elbow and hit your funny bone? That's actually another nerve, called the *ulna nerve.* It's extremely painful when you accidentally hit it.

"Well, picture taking a pair of pliers and squeezing and crushing that nerve," he said, emphasizing the word *squeezing* as he twisted an imaginary pair of pliers. "That effect would be similar to what Jesus experienced."

I winced at the image and squirmed in my chair.

"The pain was absolutely unbearable," he continued. "In fact, it was literally beyond words to describe; they had to invent a new word: *excruciating*. Literally, *excruciating* means 'out of the cross.' Think of that: they needed to create a new word because there was nothing in the language that could describe the intense anguish caused during the crucifixion.

"At this point Jesus was hoisted as the crossbar was attached to the vertical stake, and then nails were driven through Jesus' feet. Again, the nerves in his feet would have been crushed, and there would have been a similar type of pain."

Crushed and severed nerves were certainly bad enough, but I needed to know about the effect that hanging from the cross would have had on Jesus. "What stresses would this have put on his body?"

Metherell answered, "First of all, his arms would have immediately been stretched, probably about six inches in length, and both shoulders would have become dislocated—you can determine this with simple mathematical equations.

"This fulfilled the Old Testament prophecy in Psalm 22, which foretold the crucifixion hundreds of years before it took place and says, 'My bones are out of joint.'"

THE CAUSE OF DEATH

Metherell had made his point — graphically — about the pain endured as the crucifixion process began. But I needed to get to what finally claims the life of a crucifixion victim, because that's the pivotal issue in determining whether death can be faked or eluded. So I put the cause-of-death question directly to Metherell.

"Once a person is hanging in the vertical position," he replied, "crucifixion is essentially an agonizingly slow death by asphyxiation.

"The reason is that the stresses on the muscles and diaphragm put the chest into the inhaled position; basically, in order to exhale, the individual must push up on his feet so the tension on the muscles would be eased for a moment. In doing so, the nail would tear through the foot, eventually locking up against the tarsal bones.

"After managing to exhale, the person would then be able to relax down and take another breath in. Again he'd have to push himself up to exhale, scraping his bloodied back against the coarse wood of the cross. This would go on and on until complete exhaustion would take over, and the person wouldn't be able to push up and breathe anymore.

"As the person slows down his breathing, he goes into what is called *respiratory acidosis* — the carbon dioxide in the blood is dissolved as carbonic acid, causing the acidity of the blood to increase. This eventually leads to an irregular heartbeat. In fact, with his heart beating erratically, Jesus would have known that he was at the moment of death, which is when he was able to say, 'Lord, into your hands I commit my spirit.' And then he died of cardiac arrest."

It was the clearest explanation I had ever heard of death by crucifixion—but Metherell wasn't done.

"Even before he died—and this is important too—the hypovolemic shock would have caused a sustained rapid heart rate that would have contributed to heart failure, resulting in the collection of fluid in the membrane around the heart, called a *pericardial effusion,* as well as around the lungs, which is called a *pleural effusion.*"

"Why is that significant?"

"Because of what happened when the Roman soldier came around and, being fairly certain that Jesus was dead, confirmed it by thrusting a spear into his right side. It was probably his right side; that's not certain, but from the description it was probably the right side, between the ribs.

"The spear apparently went through the right lung and into the heart, so when the spear was pulled out, some fluid—the pericardial effusion and the pleural effusion—came out. This would have the appearance of a clear fluid, like water, followed by a large volume of blood, as the eyewitness John described in his gospel."

John probably had no idea why he saw both blood and a clear fluid come out—certainly that's not what an untrained person like him would have anticipated. Yet John's description is consistent with what modern medicine would expect to have happened. At first this would seem to give credibility to John being an eyewitness; however, there seemed to be one big flaw in all this.

I pulled out my Bible and flipped to John 19:34. "Wait a minute, Doc," I protested. "When you carefully read what John said, he saw 'blood and water' come out; he intentionally put the words in that order. But according to you, the clear fluid would have come out first. So there's a significant discrepancy here."

Metherell smiled slightly. "I'm not a Greek scholar," he replied, "but according to people who are, the order of words in ancient Greek was determined not necessarily by sequence but by prominence. This means that since there was a lot more blood than water, it would have made sense for John to mention the blood first."

I conceded the point but made a mental note to confirm it myself later. "At this juncture," I said, "what would Jesus' condition have been?"

Metherell's gaze locked with mine. He replied with authority, "There was absolutely no doubt that Jesus was dead."

ANSWERING THE SKEPTICS

Dr. Metherell's assertion seemed well supported by the evidence. But there were still some details I wanted to address—as well as at least one soft spot in his account that could very well undermine the credibility of the biblical account.

"The gospels say the soldiers broke the legs of the two criminals being crucified with Jesus," I said. "Why would they have done that?"

"If they wanted to speed up death—and with the Sabbath and Passover coming, the Jewish leaders certainly wanted to get this over before sundown—the Romans would use the steel shaft of a short Roman spear to shatter the victim's lower leg bones. This would prevent him from pushing up with his legs so he could breathe, and death by asphyxiation would result in a matter of minutes.

"Of course, we're told in the New Testament that Jesus' legs were not broken, because the soldiers had already determined that he was dead, and they just used the spear to confirm it. This fulfilled another Old Testament prophecy about the Messiah, which is that his bones would remain unbroken."

Again I jumped in. "Some people have tried to cast doubt on the gospel accounts by attacking the crucifixion story," I said. "For instance, an article in the *Harvard Theological Review* concluded many years ago that there was 'astonishing little evidence that the feet of a crucified person were ever pierced by nails.' Instead, the article said, the victim's hands and feet were tied to the cross by ropes.' Won't you concede that this raises credibility problems with the New Testament account?"

Dr. Metherell moved forward until he was sitting on the edge of his chair. "No," he said, "because archaeology has now established that the use of nails was historical— although I'll certainly concede that ropes were indeed sometimes used."

"What's the evidence?"

"In 1968 archaeologists in Jerusalem found the remains of about three dozen Jews who had died during the uprising against Rome around AD 70. One victim, whose name was apparently Yohanan, had been crucified. And sure enough, they found a seven-inch nail still driven into his feet, with small pieces of olive wood from the cross still attached. This was excellent archaeological confirmation of a key detail in the gospels' description of the Crucifixion."

Touché, I thought. "But one other point of dispute concerns the expertise of the Romans to determine whether Jesus was dead," I pointed out. "These people were very primitive in terms of their understanding of medicine and anatomy and so forth—how do we know they weren't just mistaken when they declared that Jesus was no longer living?"

"I'll grant you that these soldiers didn't go to medical school. But remember that they were experts in killing people—that was their job, and they did it very well. They knew without a doubt when a person was dead, and really it's not so terribly difficult to figure out.

"Besides, if a prisoner somehow escaped, the responsible soldiers would be put to death themselves, so they had a huge incentive to make absolutely sure that each and every victim was dead when he was removed from the cross."

THE FINAL ARGUMENT

Appealing to history and medicine, to archaeology and even Roman military rules, Metherell had closed every loophole: Jesus could not have come down from the cross alive. But still, I pushed him further. "Is there any possible way—*any possible way*—that Jesus could have survived this?"

Metherell shook his head and pointed his finger at me for emphasis. "Absolutely not," he said. "Remember that he was already in hypovolemic shock from the massive blood loss even before the crucifixion started. He couldn't possibly have faked his death, because you can't fake the inability to breathe for long. Besides, the spear thrust into his heart would have settled the issue once and for all.

And the Romans weren't about to risk their own death by allowing him to walk away alive."

"So," I said, "when someone suggests to you that Jesus merely swooned on the cross—"

"I tell them it's impossible. It's a fanciful theory without any possible basis in fact."

Yet I wasn't quite ready to let go of the issue. At the risk of frustrating the doctor, I said, "Let's speculate that the impossible happened and that Jesus somehow managed to survive the crucifixion. Let's say he was able to escape from his linen wrappings, roll the huge rock away from the mouth of his tomb, and get past the Roman soldiers who were standing guard. Medically speaking, what condition would he have been in after he tracked down his disciples?"

Metherell was reluctant to play that game. "Again," he stressed, becoming a bit more animated, "there's just no way he could have survived the cross.

"But if he had, how could he walk around after nails had been driven through his feet? How could he have appeared on the road to Emmaus just a short time later, strolling for long distances? How could he have used his arms after they were stretched and pulled from their joints? Remember, he also had massive wounds on his back and a spear wound to his chest."

Then he paused. Something clicked in his mind, and now he was ready to make a closing point that would drive a final stake through the heart of the swoon theory once and for all. It was an argument that nobody has been able to refute ever since it was first advanced by German theologian David Strauss in 1835.

"Listen," Metherell said, "a person in that kind of pathetic condition would never have inspired his disciples to go out and proclaim that he's the Lord of life who had triumphed over the grave.

"Do you see what I'm saying? After suffering that horrible abuse, with all the catastrophic blood loss and trauma, he would have looked so pitiful that the disciples would never have hailed him as a victorious conqueror of death; they would have felt sorry for him and tried to nurse him back to health.

"So it's preposterous to think that if he had appeared to them in that awful state, his followers would have been prompted to start a worldwide movement based on the hope that someday they too would have a resurrection body like his. There's just no way."

A QUESTION FOR THE HEART

Convincingly, masterfully, Metherell had established his case beyond a reasonable doubt. He had done it by focusing exclusively on the "how" question: How was Jesus executed in a way that absolutely ensured his death? But as we ended, I sensed that something was missing. I had tapped into his knowledge, but I hadn't touched his heart. So as we stood to shake hands, I felt compelled to ask the "why" question that begged to be posed.

"Alex, before I go, let me ask your opinion about something—not your medical opinion, not your scientific evaluation, just something from your heart."

I felt him let down his guard a bit. "Yes," he said, "I'll try."

"Jesus intentionally walked into the arms of his betrayer, he didn't resist arrest, he didn't defend himself at his trial—it was clear that he was willingly subjecting himself to what you've described as a humiliating and agonizing form of torture. And I'd like to know why. What could possibly have motivated a person to agree to endure this sort of punishment?"

Alexander Metherell—the man this time, not the doctor—searched for the right words.

"Frankly, I don't think a typical person could have done it," he finally replied. "But Jesus knew what was coming, and he was willing to go through it, because this was the only way he could redeem us—by serving as our substitute and paying the death penalty that we deserve because of our rebellion against God. That was his whole mission in coming to earth."

Having said that, I could still sense that Metherell's relentlessly rational, logical, and organized mind was continuing to crunch down my question to its most basic, nonreducible answer.

"So when you ask what motivated him," he concluded, "well ... I suppose the answer can be summed up in one word—and that would be *love*."

As I drove away that night, it was this answer that played over and over in my mind.

All in all, my interview with Metherell had been thoroughly helpful. He had persuasively established that Jesus could not have survived the ordeal of the cross, a form of cruelty so vile that the Romans exempted their own citizens from it, except for cases of high treason.

Metherell's conclusions were consistent with the findings of other physicians who have carefully studied the issue. Among them is Dr. William D. Edwards, whose

1986 article in the *Journal of the American Medical Association* concluded, "Clearly, the weight of the historical and medical evidence indicates that Jesus was dead before the wound to his side was inflicted.... Accordingly, interpretations based on the assumption that Jesus did not die on the cross appear to be at odds with modern medical knowledge."[10]

Those who seek to explain away the resurrection of Jesus by claiming that he somehow escaped the clutches of death at Golgotha need to offer a more plausible theory that fits the facts.

And then they too must end up pondering the haunting question that all of us need to consider: What could possibly have motivated Jesus to willingly allow himself to be degraded and brutalized the way that he did?

DELIBERATIONS
Questions for Reflection or Group Study

1. After considering Dr. Metherell's account, do you see any validity to the swoon theory? Why or why not?
2. For two millennia the cross has been a symbol for Christians. Now that you've read Metherell's testimony, how might your own view of that symbol be different in the future?
3. Would you be willing to suffer for the sake of another person? For whom and why? What would it take to motivate you to endure torture in the place of someone else?

4. How would you react to the soldiers if they were abusing, humiliating, and torturing you, as they did Jesus? What could possibly account for Jesus' reaction, which was to utter in the midst of his agony, "Father, forgive them"?

THE EVIDENCE OF THE MISSING BODY: WAS JESUS' BODY REALLY ABSENT FROM HIS TOMB?

Candy heiress Helen Vorhees Brach flew into O'Hare International Airport on a crisp autumn afternoon, stepped into a crowd, and promptly disappeared without a trace. For more than twenty years the mystery of what happened to this red-haired, animal-loving philanthropist has baffled police and journalists alike.

While investigators are convinced she was murdered, they haven't been able to determine the specific circumstances, largely because they've never found her body. Police have floated some speculation, leaked tantalizing possibilities to the press, and even got a judge to declare that a con man was responsible for her disappearance. But absent a corpse, her murder officially remains unsolved. Nobody has ever been charged with her slaying.

The Brach case is one of those frustrating enigmas that keep me awake from time to time as I mentally sift through the sparse evidence and try to piece together what happened. Ultimately it's an unsatisfying exercise; I want to *know* what happened, and there just aren't enough facts to chase away the conjecture.

Occasionally bodies turn up missing in pulp fiction and real life, but rarely do you encounter an empty tomb. Unlike the case of Helen Brach, the issue with Jesus isn't that he was nowhere to be seen. It's that he *was* seen, alive; he *was* seen, dead; and he *was* seen, alive once more. If we believe the gospel accounts, this isn't a matter of a missing body. No, it's a matter of Jesus still being alive, even to this day, even after publicly succumbing to the horrors of crucifixion so graphically depicted in the preceding chapter.

The empty tomb, as an enduring symbol of the resurrection, is the ultimate representation of Jesus' claim to being God. The apostle Paul said in 1 Corinthians 15:17 that the resurrection is at the very core of the Christian faith: "If Christ has not been raised, your faith is futile; you are still in your sins."

Theologian Gerald O'Collins put it this way: "In a profound sense, Christianity without the resurrection is not simply Christianity without its final chapter. It is not Christianity at all."[1]

The resurrection is the supreme vindication of Jesus' divine identity and his inspired teaching. It's the proof of his triumph over sin and death. It's the foreshadowing of the resurrection of his followers. It's the basis of Christian hope. It's the miracle of all miracles.

If it's true. Skeptics claim that what happened to Jesus' body is still a mystery akin to Helen Brach's disappearance—there's not enough evidence, they say, to reach a firm conclusion.

But others assert that the case is effectively closed because there is conclusive proof that the tomb was vacant on that first Easter morning. And if you want someone to compellingly present that case, your best bet is to visit with William Lane Craig, widely considered to be among the world's foremost experts on the resurrection.

INTERVIEW WITH WILLIAM LANE CRAIG, PH.D., D.TH.

I had an unusual perspective the first time I saw Bill Craig in action: I was seated behind him as he defended Christianity before a crowd of nearly eight thousand people, with countless others listening on more than one hundred radio stations across the country.

As moderator of a debate between Craig and an atheist selected by the national spokesman for American Atheists, Inc., I marveled as Craig politely but powerfully built the case for Christianity while simultaneously dismantling the arguments for atheism. From where I was sitting, I could watch the faces of people as they discovered — many for the first time — that Christianity can stand up to rational analysis and rugged scrutiny.

In the end it was no contest. Among those who had entered the auditorium that evening as avowed atheists, agnostics, or skeptics, an overwhelming 82 percent walked out concluding that the case for Christianity had been the most compelling. Forty-seven people entered as nonbelievers and exited as Christians — Craig's arguments for the faith were that persuasive, especially compared with the paucity of evidence for atheism. Incidentally, I know of nobody who became an atheist.[2]

So when I flew down to Atlanta to interview him, I was anxious to see how he'd respond to the challenges concerning the empty tomb of Jesus.

Craig hadn't changed since I had seen him a few years earlier. With his close-cropped black beard, angular features, and riveting gaze, Craig still looks the role of a serious scholar. He speaks in cogent sentences, never losing his train of thought, always working through an answer methodically, point by point, fact by fact.

Yet he isn't a dry theologian. Craig has a refreshing enthusiasm for his work. His pale blue eyes dance as he weaves elaborate propositions and theories; he punctuates his sentences with hand gestures that beckon for understanding and agreement; his voice modulates from near giddiness over some arcane theological point that he finds fascinating to hushed sincerity as he ponders why some scholars resist the evidence that he finds so powerful.

In short, his mind is fully engaged, but so is his heart. When he talks about skeptics he has debated, it isn't with a smug or adversarial tone. He goes out of his way to mention their endearing qualities when he can — this one was a wonderful speaker, that one was charming over dinner.

In the subtleties of our conversation, I sensed that he isn't out to pummel opponents with his arguments; he's sincerely seeking to win over people who he believes matter to God. He seems genuinely perplexed why some people cannot, or will not, recognize the reality of the empty tomb.

DEFENDING THE EMPTY TOMB

Wearing blue jeans, white socks, and a dark-blue sweater with red turtleneck collar, Craig lounged on a floral couch in his living room. On the wall behind him was a large framed scene of Munich.

It was there, fresh with a master of arts degree from Trinity Evangelical Divinity School and a doctorate in philosophy from the University of Birmingham, England, that Craig studied the resurrection for the first time, while earning another doctorate, this one in theology from the University of Munich. He later taught at Trinity Evangelical Divinity School and then served as a visiting scholar at the Higher Institute of Philosophy at the University of Louvain near Brussels.

His books include *Reasonable Faith*; *No Easy Answers*; *Knowing the Truth about the Resurrection*; *The Only Wise God*; *The Existence of God and the Beginning of the Universe*; and (with Quentin Smith) *Theism, Atheism, and Big Bang Cosmology*, published by Oxford University Press.

He also contributed to *The Intellectuals Speak Out about God*; *Jesus under Fire*; *In Defense of Miracles*; and *Does God Exist?* In addition, his scholarly articles have appeared in such journals as *New Testament Studies; Journal for the Study of the New Testament; Gospel Perspectives; Journal of the American Scientific Affiliation*; and *Philosophy*. He is a member of nine professional societies, including the American Academy of Religion and the American Philosophical Association.

While he is internationally known for his writings about the intersection of science, philosophy, and theology, he needed no prompting to discuss the subject that still makes his heart beat fast: the resurrection of Jesus.

WAS JESUS REALLY BURIED IN THE TOMB?

Before looking at whether the tomb of Jesus was empty, I needed to establish whether his body had been there in the first place. History tells us that as a rule, crucified criminals were left on the cross to be devoured by birds or were thrown into a common grave. This has prompted John Dominic Crossan of the liberal Jesus Seminar to conclude that Jesus' body probably was dug up and consumed by wild dogs.

"Based on these customary practices," I said to Craig, "wouldn't you admit that this is most likely what happened?"

"If all you looked at was customary practice, yes, I'd agree," came his reply. "But that would ignore the specific evidence in this case."

"Okay, then let's look at the specific evidence," I said. With that I pointed out an immediate problem: the gospels say Jesus' corpse was turned over to Joseph of Arimathea, a member of the very council—the Sanhedrin—that voted to condemn Jesus. "That's rather implausible, isn't it?" I demanded in a tone that sounded more pointed than I had intended.

Craig shifted on the couch as if he were getting ready to pounce on my question. "No, not when you look at all the evidence for the burial," he said. "So let me go through it. For one thing, the burial is mentioned by the apostle Paul in 1 Corinthians 15:3–7, where he passes on a very early creed of the church."

Craig agrees with various scholars that this creed—a statement that Christians would recite to summarize their beliefs—undoubtedly goes back to within a few years of Jesus' crucifixion, having been given to Paul, after his conversion, in Damascus or in his subsequent visit to Jerusalem when he met with the apostles James and Peter.

Since Craig was going to be referring to the creed, I opened the Bible in my lap and quickly reviewed the passage: "For what I received I passed on to you as of first importance: that Christ died for our sins according to the

Scriptures, that he was buried, that he was raised on the third day according to the Scriptures ..." The creed then goes on to list several appearances of the resurrected Jesus.

"This creed is incredibly early and therefore trustworthy material," Craig said. "Essentially, it's a four-line formula. The first line refers to the crucifixion, the second to the burial, the third to the resurrection, and the fourth to Jesus' appearances. As you can see, the second line affirms that Jesus was buried."

That was too vague for me. "Wait a minute," I interjected. "He may have been buried, but was it in a tomb? And was it through Joseph of Arimathea, this mysterious character who comes out of nowhere to claim the body?"

Craig remained patient. "This creed is actually a summary that corresponds line by line with what the gospels teach," he explained. "When we turn to the gospels, we find multiple, independent attestation of this burial story, and Joseph of Arimathea is specifically named in all four accounts. On top of that, the burial story in Mark is so extremely early that it's simply not possible for it to have been subject to legendary corruption."

"How can you tell it's early?" I asked.

"Two reasons," he said. "First, Mark is generally considered to be the earliest gospel. Second, his gospel basically consists of short anecdotes about Jesus, more like pearls on a string than a smooth, continuous narrative.

"But when you get to the last week of Jesus' life—the so-called passion story—then you do have a continuous narrative of events in sequence. This passion story was apparently taken by Mark from an even earlier source—and this source included the story of Jesus being buried in the tomb."

IS JOSEPH OF ARIMATHEA HISTORICAL?

While those were good arguments, I spotted a problem with Mark's account of what happened. "Mark says that the entire Sanhedrin voted to condemn Jesus," I said. "If that's true, this means Joseph of Arimathea cast his ballot to kill Jesus. Isn't it highly unlikely that he would have then come to give Jesus an honorable burial?"

Apparently, my observation put me in good company. "Luke may have felt this same discomfort," Craig said, "which would explain why he added one important detail—Joseph of Arimathea wasn't present when the official vote was taken. So that would explain things. But the significant point about Joseph of Arimathea is that he would not be the sort of person who would have been invented by Christian legend or Christian authors."

I needed more than merely a conclusion on that matter; I wanted some solid reasoning. "Why not?" I asked.

"Given the early Christian anger and bitterness toward the Jewish leaders who had instigated the crucifixion of Jesus," he said, "it's highly improbable that they would have invented one who did the right thing by giving Jesus an honorable burial—especially while all of Jesus' disciples deserted him! Besides, they wouldn't make up a specific member of a specific group, whom people could check out for themselves and ask about this. So Joseph is undoubtedly a historical figure."

Before I could ask a follow-up question, Craig continued. "I'll add that if this burial by Joseph were a legend that developed later, you'd expect to find other competing burial traditions about what happened to Jesus' body. However, you don't find these at all.

"As a result, the majority of New Testament scholars today agree that the burial account of Jesus is fundamentally reliable. John A. T. Robinson, the late Cambridge University New Testament scholar, said the honorable burial of Jesus is one of the earliest and best-attested facts that we have about the historical Jesus."

Craig's explanations satisfied me that Jesus' body was indeed placed in Joseph's tomb. But the creed left an ambiguity: perhaps, even after the resurrection, his body remained entombed.

"While the creed says Jesus was crucified, buried, and then resurrected, it doesn't specifically say the tomb was empty," I pointed out. "Doesn't this leave room for the possibility that the resurrection was only spiritual in nature and that Jesus' body was still in the tomb?"

"The creed definitely implies the empty tomb," Craig countered. "You see, the Jews had a physical concept of resurrection. For them, the primary object of the resurrection was the bones of the deceased—not even the flesh, which was thought to be perishable. After the flesh rotted away, the Jews would gather the bones of their deceased and put them in boxes to be preserved until the resurrection at the end of the world, when God would raise the righteous dead of Israel and they would come together in the final kingdom of God.

"In light of this, it would have been simply a contradiction of terms for an early Jew to say that someone was raised from the dead but his body still was left in the tomb.

So when this early Christian creed says Jesus was buried and then raised on the third day, it's saying implicitly but quite clearly: an empty tomb was left behind."

HOW SECURE WAS THE TOMB?

Having heard convincing evidence that Jesus had been in the tomb, it seemed important to know how secure his grave was from outside influences. The tighter the security, the less likely the body could have been tampered with. "How protected was Jesus' tomb?" I asked.

Craig proceeded to describe how this kind of tomb looked, as best as archaeologists have been able to determine from excavations of first-century sites.

"There was a slanted groove that led down to a low entrance, and a large disk-shaped stone was rolled down this groove and lodged into place across the door," he said, using his hands to illustrate what he was saying. "A smaller stone was then used to secure the disk. Although it would be easy to roll this big disk down the groove, it would take several men to roll the stone back up in order to reopen the tomb. In that sense it was quite secure."

However, was Jesus' tomb also guarded? I knew that some skeptics have attempted to cast doubt on the popular belief that Jesus' tomb was carefully watched around the clock by highly disciplined Roman soldiers, who faced death themselves if they failed in their duty.

"Are you convinced there were Roman guards?" I asked.

"Only Matthew reports that guards were placed around the tomb," he replied. "But in any event, I don't think the guard story is an important facet of the evidence for the resurrection. For one thing, it's too disputed by contemporary scholarship. I find it's prudent to base my arguments on evidence that's most widely accepted by the majority of scholars, so the guard story is better left aside."

I was surprised by his approach. "Doesn't that weaken your case?" I asked.

Craig shook his head. "Frankly, the guard story may have been important in the eighteenth century, when critics were suggesting that the disciples stole Jesus' body, but nobody espouses that theory today," he responded.

"When you read the New Testament," he continued, "there's no doubt that the disciples sincerely believed the truth of the resurrection, which they proclaimed to their deaths. The idea that the empty tomb is the result of some hoax, conspiracy, or theft is simply dismissed today. So the guard story has become sort of incidental."

WERE ANY GUARDS PRESENT?

Even so, I was interested in whether there was any evidence to back up Matthew's assertion about the guards. Although I understood Craig's reasons for setting aside the issue, I pressed ahead by asking whether there was any good evidence that the guard story is historical.

"Yes, there is," he said. "Think about the claims and counterclaims about the resurrection that went back and forth between the Jews and Christians in the first century.

"The initial Christian proclamation was, 'Jesus is risen.' The Jews responded, 'The disciples stole his body.' To this Christians said, 'Ah, but the guards at the tomb would have prevented such a theft.' The Jews responded, 'Oh, but the guards at the tomb fell asleep.' To that the Christians replied, 'No, the Jews bribed the guards to say they fell asleep.'

"Now, if there had not been any guards, the exchange would have gone like this: In response to the claim Jesus is risen, the Jews would say, 'No, the disciples stole his body.' Christians would reply, 'But the guards would have prevented the theft.' Then the Jewish response would have been, 'What guards? You're crazy! There were no guards!' Yet history tells us that's not what the Jews said.

"This suggests the guards really were historical and that the Jews knew it, which is why they had to invent the absurd story about the guards having been asleep while the disciples took the body."

Again a nagging question prompted me to jump in. "There seems to be another problem here," I said, pausing as I tried to formulate my objection as succinctly as I could.

"Why would the Jewish authorities have placed guards at the tomb in the first place? If they were anticipating a resurrection or the disciples faking one, this would mean they had a better understanding of Jesus' predictions about his resurrection than the disciples did! After all, the disciples were surprised by the whole thing."

"You've hit on something there," Craig conceded. "However, maybe they placed the guards there to prevent any sort of tomb robbery or other disturbances from happening during Passover. We don't know. That's a good argument; I grant its full force. But I don't think it's insuperable."

Yes, but it does raise some question concerning the guard story. Plus another objection came to mind. "Matthew says the Roman guards reported to the Jewish authorities," I said.

"But doesn't that seem unlikely, since they were responsible to Pilate?"

A slight smile came to Craig's face. "If you look carefully," he said, "Matthew doesn't say the guards are Romans. When the Jews go to Pilate and ask for a guard, Pilate says, 'You have a guard.' Now, does he mean, 'All right, here's a detachment of Roman soldiers'? Or does he mean, 'You've got your own temple guards; use them'?

"Scholars have debated whether or not it was a Jewish guard. I was initially inclined, for the reason you mentioned, to think that the guard was Jewish. I've rethought that, however, because the word Matthew uses to refer to the guards is often used with respect to Roman soldiers rather than just temple officers.

"And remember, John tells us it was a Roman centurion who led Roman soldiers to arrest Jesus under the direction of Jewish leadership. So there is precedent for Roman guards reporting to Jewish religious leaders. It seems plausible that they could also be involved in the guarding of the tomb."

Weighing the evidence, I felt persuaded that guards had been present, but I decided to drop this line of questioning, since Craig doesn't rely on the guard story anyway. Meanwhile I was anxious to confront Craig with what seems to be the most persuasive argument against the idea that Jesus' tomb was vacant on Easter Morning.

WHAT ABOUT THE CONTRADICTIONS?

Through the years, critics of Christianity have attacked the empty tomb story by pointing out apparent discrepancies among the gospel accounts. For example, skeptic Charles Templeton said, "The four descriptions of events ... differ so markedly at so many points that, with all the good will in the world, they cannot be reconciled."[3]

Taken at face value, this objection seems to penetrate to the heart of the reliability of the empty tomb narratives. Consider this summary by Dr. Michael Martin of Boston University, which I read to Craig that morning:

> In Matthew, when Mary Magdalene and the other Mary arrived toward dawn at the tomb there is a rock in front of it, there is a violent earthquake, and an angel descends and rolls back the stone. In Mark, the women arrive at the tomb at sunrise and the stone had been rolled back. In Luke, when the women arrive at early dawn they find the stone had already been rolled back.
>
> In Matthew, an angel is sitting on the rock outside the tomb and in Mark a youth is inside the tomb. In Luke, two men are inside.
>
> In Matthew, the women present at the tomb are Mary Magdalene and the other Mary. In Mark, the women present at the tomb are the two Marys and Salome. In Luke, Mary Magdalene, Mary the mother of James, Joanna, and the other women are present at the tomb.
>
> In Matthew, the two Marys rush from the tomb in great fear and joy, run to tell the disciples, and meet Jesus on the way. In Mark, they run out of the tomb in fear and say nothing to anyone. In Luke, the women report the story to

the disciples who do not believe them and there is no suggestion that they meet Jesus.[4]

"And," I said to Craig, "Martin points out that John conflicts with much of the other three gospels. He concludes, 'In sum, the accounts of what happened at the tomb are either inconsistent or can only be made consistent with the aid of implausible interpretations.' "[5]

I stopped reading and looked up from my notes. My eyes locking with Craig's, I asked him point-blank, "In light of all this, how in the world can you possibly consider the empty tomb story to be credible?"

Immediately I noticed something about Craig's demeanor. In casual conversation or when discussing tepid objections to the empty tomb, he's rather mellow. But the tougher the question and the more piercing the challenge, the more animated and focused he gets. And at this point his body language told me he couldn't wait to dive into these seemingly dangerous waters.

Clearing his throat, Craig began. "With all due respect," he said, "Michael Martin is a philosopher, not a historian, and I don't think he understands the historian's craft. For a philosopher, if something is inconsistent, the law of contradiction says, 'This cannot be true, throw it out!' However, the historian looks at these narratives and says, 'I see some inconsistencies, but I notice something about them: they're all in the secondary details.'

"The core of the story is the same: Joseph of Arimathea takes the body of Jesus, puts it in a tomb, the tomb is visited by a small group of women followers of Jesus early on the Sunday morning following his crucifixion, and they find that the tomb is empty. They see a vision of angels saying that Jesus is risen.

"The careful historian, unlike the philosopher, doesn't throw out the baby with the bath water. He says, 'This suggests that there is a historical core to this story that is reliable and can be depended upon, however conflicting the secondary details might be.'

"So we can have great confidence in the core that's common to the narratives and that would be agreed upon by the majority of New Testament scholars today, even if there are some differences concerning the names of the women, the exact time of the morning, the number of the angels, and so forth. Those kinds of secondary discrepancies wouldn't bother a historian."

Even the usually skeptical historian Michael Grant, a fellow of Trinity College, Cambridge, and professor at Edinburgh University, concedes in his book *Jesus: An Historian's Review of the Gospels*, "True, the discovery of the empty tomb is differently described by the various gospels, but if we apply the same sort of criteria that we would apply to any other ancient literary sources, then the evidence is firm and plausible enough to necessitate the conclusion that the tomb was, indeed, found empty."[6]

CAN DISCREPANCIES BE HARMONIZED?

Sometimes while covering criminal trials, I've seen two witnesses give the exact same testimony, down to the nitty-gritty details, only to find themselves ripped apart by the defense attorney for having colluded before the trial. So I remarked to Craig, "I suppose if all four gospels were identical in all their minutiae, that would have raised the suspicion of plagiarism."

"Yes, that's a very good point," he said. "The differences between the empty tomb narratives suggest that we have multiple, independent attestations of the empty tomb story. Sometimes people say, 'Matthew and Luke just plagiarized from Mark,' but when you look at the narratives closely, you see divergences that suggest that even if Matthew and Luke did know Mark's account, nevertheless they also had separate, independent sources for the empty tomb story.

"So with these multiple and independent accounts, no historian would disregard this evidence just because of secondary discrepancies. Let me give you a secular example.

"We have two narratives of Hannibal crossing the Alps to attack Rome, and they're incompatible and irreconcilable. Yet no classical historian doubts the fact that Hannibal did mount such a campaign. That's a nonbiblical illustration of discrepancies in secondary details failing to undermine the historical core of a historical story."

I conceded the power of that argument. And as I reflected on Martin's critique, it seemed to me that some of his alleged contradictions could be rather easily reconciled. I mentioned this to Craig by saying, "Aren't there ways to harmonize some of the differences among these accounts?"

"Yes, that's right, there are," Craig replied. "For example, the time of the visit to the tomb. One writer might describe it as still being dark, the other might be saying it was getting light, but that's sort of like the optimist and the pessimist arguing over whether the glass was half empty or half full. It was around dawn, and they were describing the same thing with different words.

"As for the number and names of the women, none of the gospels pretend to give a complete list. They all include Mary Magdalene and other women, so there was probably a gaggle of these early disciples that included those who were named and probably a couple of others. I think it would be pedantic to say that's a contradiction."

"What about the different accounts of what happened afterward?" I asked. "Mark said the women didn't tell anybody, and the other gospels say they did."

Craig explained, "When you look at Mark's theology, he loves to emphasize awe and fright and terror and worship in the presence of the divine. So this reaction of the women—of fleeing with fear and trembling, and saying nothing to anyone because they were afraid—is all part of Mark's literary and theological style.

"It could well be that this was a temporary silence, and then the women went back and told the others what had happened. In fact," he concluded with a grin, "it *had* to be a temporary silence; otherwise Mark couldn't be telling the story about it!"

I wanted to ask about one other commonly cited discrepancy. "Jesus said in Matthew 12:40, 'For as Jonah was three days and three nights in the belly of a huge fish, so the Son of Man will be three days and three nights in the heart of the earth.' However, the gospels report that Jesus was really in the tomb one full day, two full nights, and part of two days. Isn't this an example of Jesus being wrong in not fulfilling his own prophecy?"

"Some well-meaning Christians have used this verse to suggest Jesus was crucified on Wednesday rather than on Friday, in order to get the full time in there!" Craig said. "But most scholars recognize that according to early Jewish time-reckoning, any part of a day counted as a full day. Jesus was in the tomb Friday afternoon, all day Saturday, and on Sunday morning—under the way the Jews conceptualized time back then, this would have counted as three days.[7]

"Again," he concluded, "that's just another example of how many of these discrepancies can be explained or minimized with some background knowledge or by just thinking them through with an open mind."

CAN THE WITNESSES BE TRUSTED?

The gospels agree that the empty tomb was discovered by women who were friends and followers of Jesus. But that, in Michael Martin's estimation, makes their testimony suspect, since they were "probably not objective observers."

So I put the question to Craig: "Does the women's relationship with Jesus call the reliability of their testimony into question?"

Unwittingly I had played right into Craig's hand. "Actually, this argument backfires on people who use it," Craig said in response. "Certainly these women were friends of Jesus. But when you understand the role of women in first-century Jewish society, what's really extraordinary is that this empty tomb story should feature women as the discoverers of the empty tomb in the first place.

"Women were on a very low rung of the social ladder in first-century Palestine. There are old rabbinical sayings that said, 'Let the words of the Law be burned rather than delivered to women' and 'Blessed is he whose children are male, but woe to him whose children are female.' Women's testimony was regarded as so worthless that they weren't even allowed to serve as legal witnesses in a Jewish court of law.

"In light of this, it's absolutely remarkable that the chief witnesses to the empty tomb are these women who were friends of Jesus. Any later legendary account would have certainly portrayed male disciples as discovering the tomb—Peter or John, for example. The fact that women are the first witnesses to the empty tomb is most plausibly explained by the reality that—like it or not—they *were* the discoverers of the empty tomb! This shows that the gospel writers faithfully recorded what happened, even if it was embarrassing. This bespeaks the historicity of this tradition rather than its legendary status."

WHY DID THE WOMEN VISIT THE TOMB?

Craig's explanation, however, left yet another question lingering: Why were the women going to anoint the body of Jesus if they already knew that his tomb was securely sealed? "Do their actions really make sense?" I asked.

Craig thought for a moment before he answered—this time not in his debater's voice but in a more tender tone. "Lee, I strongly feel that scholars who have not known the love and devotion that these women felt for Jesus have no right to pronounce cool judgments upon the feasibility of what they wanted to do.

"For people who are grieving, who have lost someone they desperately loved and followed, to want to go to the tomb in a forlorn hope of anointing the body—I just don't think some later critic can treat them like robots and say, 'They shouldn't have gone.'"

He shrugged his shoulders. "Maybe they thought there would be men around who could move the stone. If there were guards, maybe they thought they would. I don't know.

"Certainly the notion of visiting a tomb to pour oils over a body is a historical Jewish practice; the only question is the feasibility of who would move the stone for them. And I don't think we're in the right position to pronounce judgment on whether or not they should have simply stayed at home."

WHY DIDN'T CHRISTIANS CITE THE EMPTY TOMB?

In preparing for my interview with Craig, I had heard more than one skeptic claim that a major argument against the empty tomb is that none of the apostles, including Peter, bothered to point to it in their preaching. But when I asked Craig about this issue, his eyes widened.

"I just don't think that's true," he replied, a bit of astonishment in his voice, as he picked up his Bible and turned to the second chapter of Acts, which records Peter's sermon at Pentecost.

"The empty tomb *is* found in Peter's speech," Craig insisted. "He proclaims in verse 24 that 'God raised him from the dead, freeing him from the agony of death.'

"Then he quotes from a psalm about how God would not allow his Holy One to undergo decay. This had been written by David, and Peter says, 'I can tell you confidently that the patriarch David died and was buried, and his tomb is here to this day.' But, he says, Christ 'was not abandoned to the grave, nor did his body see decay. God has raised this Jesus to life, and we are all witnesses of the fact.'"

Craig looked up from the Bible. "This speech contrasts David's tomb, which remained to that day, with the prophecy in which David says Christ would be raised up—his flesh wouldn't suffer decay. It's clearly implicit that the tomb was left empty."

Then he turned to a later chapter in the book of Acts. "In Acts 13:29–31, Paul says, 'When they had carried out all that was written about him, they took him down from the tree and laid him in a tomb. But God raised him from the dead, and for many days he was seen by those who had traveled with him from Galilee to Jerusalem.' Certainly the empty tomb is implicit there."

He shut his Bible, then added, "I think it's rather wooden and unreasonable to contend that these early preachers didn't refer to the empty tomb, just because they didn't use the two specific words *empty tomb*. There's no question that they knew—and their audiences understood from their preaching—that Jesus' tomb was vacant."

WHAT'S THE AFFIRMATIVE EVIDENCE?

I had spent the first part of our interview peppering Craig with objections and arguments challenging the empty tomb. But I suddenly realized that I hadn't given him the opportunity to spell out his affirmative case. While he had already alluded to several reasons why he believes Jesus' tomb was unoccupied, I said, "Why don't you give me your best shot? Convince me with your top four or five reasons that the empty tomb is a historical fact."

Craig rose to the challenge. One by one he spelled out his arguments concisely and powerfully.

"First," he said, "the empty tomb is definitely implicit in the early tradition that is passed along by Paul in 1 Corinthians 15, which is a very old and reliable source of historical information about Jesus.

"Second, the site of Jesus' tomb was known to Christian and Jew alike. So if it weren't empty, it would be impossible for a movement founded on belief in the resurrection to have come into existence in the same city where this man had been publicly executed and buried.

"Third, we can tell from the language, grammar, and style that Mark got his empty tomb story—actually, his whole passion narrative—from an earlier source. In fact, there's evidence it was written before AD 37, which is much too early for legend to have seriously corrupted it.

"A. N. Sherwin-White, the respected Greco-Roman classical historian from Oxford University, said it would have been without precedent anywhere in history for legend to have grown up that fast and significantly distorted the gospels.

"Fourth, there's the simplicity of the empty tomb story in Mark. Fictional apocryphal accounts from the second century contain all kinds of flowery narratives, in which Jesus comes out of the tomb in glory and power, with

everybody seeing him, including the priests, Jewish authorities, and Roman guards. Those are the way legends read,
but these don't come until generations after the events,
which is after eyewitnesses have died off. By contrast,
Mark's account of the story of the empty tomb is stark
in its simplicity and unadorned by theological reflection.

"Fifth, the unanimous testimony that the empty tomb
was discovered by women argues for the authenticity of
the story, because this would have been embarrassing for
the disciples to admit and most certainly would have been
covered up if this were a legend.

"Sixth, the earliest Jewish polemic presupposes the
historicity of the empty tomb. In other words, there was
nobody who was claiming that the tomb still contained
Jesus' body. The question always was, 'What happened
to the body?'

"The Jews proposed the ridiculous story that the
guards had fallen asleep. Obviously, they were grasp-
ing at straws. But the point is this: they started with the
assumption that the tomb was vacant! Why? Because they
knew it was!"

WHAT ABOUT ALTERNATIVE THEORIES?

I listened intently as Craig articulated each point, and
to me the six arguments added up to an impressive case.
I still wanted to see if there were any loopholes, however,
before concluding it was airtight.

"Kirsopp Lake suggested in 1907 that the women
merely went to the wrong tomb," I said. "He says they
got lost and a caretaker at an unoccupied tomb told them,

'You're looking for Jesus of Nazareth. He is not here,' and they ran away, afraid. Isn't that a plausible explanation?"[8]

Craig sighed. "Lake didn't generate any following with this," he said. "The reason is that the site of Jesus' tomb was known to the Jewish authorities. Even if the women had made this mistake, the authorities would have been only too happy to point out the tomb and correct the disciples' error when they began to proclaim that Jesus had risen from the dead. I don't know anybody who holds to Lake's theory today."

Frankly, other options didn't sound very likely, either. Obviously, the disciples had no motive to steal the body and then die for a lie, and certainly the Jewish authorities wouldn't have removed the body. I said, "We're left with the theory that the empty tomb was a later legend and that by the time it developed, people were unable to disprove it, because the location of the tomb had been forgotten."

"That has been the issue ever since 1835, when David Strauss claimed these stories are legendary," Craig replied. "And that's why in our conversation today we've focused so much on this legendary hypothesis by showing that the empty tomb story goes back to within a few years of the events themselves. This renders the legend theory worthless. Even if there are some legendary elements in the secondary details of the story, the historical core of the story remains securely established."

Yes, there were answers for these alternative explanations. Upon analysis, every theory seemed to crumble under the weight of evidence and logic. But the only remaining option was to believe that the crucified Jesus returned to life—a conclusion some people find too extraordinary to swallow.

I thought for a moment about how I could phrase this in a question to Craig. Finally I said, "Even though these alternative theories admittedly have holes in them, aren't they more plausible than the absolutely incredible idea that Jesus was God incarnate who was raised from the dead?"

"This, I think, is the issue," he said, leaning forward. "I think people who push these alternative theories would admit, 'Yes, our theories are implausible, but they're not as improbable as the idea that this spectacular miracle occurred.' At this point, however, the matter is no longer a historical issue; instead it's a philosophical question about whether miracles are possible."

"And what," I asked, "would you say to that?"

"I would argue that the hypothesis that God raised Jesus from the dead is not at all improbable. In fact, based on the evidence, it's the best explanation for what happened. What is improbable is the hypothesis that Jesus rose naturally from the dead. That, I would agree, is outlandish. Any hypothesis would be more probable than saying the corpse of Jesus spontaneously came back to life.

"But the hypothesis that God raised Jesus from the dead doesn't contradict science or any known facts of experience. All it requires is the hypothesis that God exists, and I think there are good independent reasons for believing that he does."

With that Craig added this clincher: "As long as the existence of God is even possible, it's possible that he acted in history by raising Jesus from the dead."

CONCLUSION: THE TOMB WAS VACANT

Craig was convincing: the empty tomb—admittedly, a miracle of staggering proportions—did make sense in light of the evidence. And it was only part of the case for the resurrection. From Craig's Atlanta home I was getting ready to go to Virginia to interview a renowned expert on the evidence for the appearances of the resurrected Jesus.

As I thanked Craig and his wife, Jan, for their hospitality, I reflected to myself that up close, in his blue jeans and white socks, Craig didn't look like the kind of formidable adversary who would devastate the best resurrection critics in the world. But I had heard the tapes of the debates for myself.

In the face of the facts, they have been impotent to put Jesus' body back into the tomb. They flounder, they struggle, they snatch at straws, they contradict themselves, they pursue desperate and extraordinary theories to try to account for the evidence. Yet each time, in the end, the tomb remains vacant.

I was reminded of the assessment by one of the towering legal intellects of all time, the Cambridge-educated Sir Norman Anderson, who lectured at Princeton University, was offered a professorship for life at Harvard University, and served as dean of the Faculty of Laws at the University of London. His conclusion, after a lifetime of analyzing this issue from a legal perspective, was summed up in one sentence: "The empty tomb, then, forms a veritable rock on which all rationalistic theories of the resurrection dash themselves in vain."[9]

DELIBERATIONS
Questions for Reflection or Group Study

1. What's your own conclusion concerning whether Jesus' tomb was empty on Easter Morning? What evidence did you find most convincing in coming to that judgment?

2. As Craig pointed out, everyone in the ancient world admitted the tomb was empty; the issue was how it got that way. Can you think of any logical explanation for the vacant tomb other than the resurrection of Jesus? If so, how do you imagine someone like Bill Craig might respond to your theory?

3. Read Mark 15:42–16:8, the earliest account of Jesus' burial and empty tomb. Do you agree with Craig that it is "stark in its simplicity and unadorned by theological reflection"? Why or why not?

THE EVIDENCE OF APPEARANCES: WAS JESUS SEEN ALIVE AFTER HIS DEATH ON THE CROSS?

In 1963 the body of fourteen-year-old Addie Mae Collins, one of four African-American girls tragically murdered in an infamous church bombing by white racists, was buried in Birmingham, Alabama. For years family members kept returning to the grave to pray and leave flowers. In 1998 they made the decision to disinter the deceased for reburial at another cemetery.

When workers were sent to dig up the body, however, they returned with a shocking discovery: The grave was empty.

Understandably, family members were terribly distraught. Hampered by poorly kept records, cemetery officials scrambled to figure out what had happened. Several possibilities were raised, the primary one being that her tombstone had been erected in the wrong place.[1]

Yet in the midst of determining what happened, one explanation was never proposed: Nobody suggested that young Addie Mae had been resurrected to walk the earth again. Why? Because by itself an empty grave does not a resurrection make.

My conversation with Dr. William Lane Craig has already elicited powerful evidence that the tomb of Jesus was empty the Sunday after his crucifixion. While I knew that this was important and necessary evidence for his resurrection, I was also aware that a missing body is not conclusive proof by itself. More facts would be needed to establish that Jesus really did return from the dead.

That's what prompted my plane trip to Virginia. As my flight gently banked over the wooded hills below, I was doing some last-minute reading of a book by Michael Martin, the Boston University professor who has sought to discredit Christianity. I smiled at his words: "Perhaps the most sophisticated defense of the resurrection to date has been produced by Gary Habermas."[2]

I glanced at my watch. I would land with just enough time to rent a car, drive to Lynchburg, and make my two o'clock appointment with Habermas himself.

INTERVIEW WITH GARY HABERMAS, PH.D., D.D.

Two autographed photos of hockey players, shown in flat-out combat on ice, hang on the walls of Habermas's austere office. One features the immortal Bobby Hull of the Chicago Blackhawks; the other depicts Dave "The Hammer" Schultz, the brawling, tough-as-nails forward for the Philadelphia Flyers.

"Hull is my favorite hockey player," explains Habermas. "Schultz is my favorite fighter." He grinned, then added, "There's a difference."

Habermas—bearded, straight-talking, rough-hewn—is also a fighter, an academic pit bull who looks more like a nightclub bouncer than an ivory tower intellectual. Armed with razor-sharp arguments and historical evidence to back them up, he's not afraid to come out swinging.

Antony Flew, one of the leading philosophical atheists in the world, found that out when he tangled with Habermas in a major debate on the topic "Did Jesus Rise from the Dead?" The results were decidedly one-sided. Of the five independent philosophers from various colleges and universities who served as judges of the debate's content, four concluded that Habermas had won. One called the contest a draw. None cast a ballot for Flew. Commented one judge, "I was surprised (shocked might be a more accurate word) to see how weak Flew's own approach was.... I was left with this conclusion: Since the case against the resurrection was no stronger than that presented by Antony Flew, I would think it was time I began to take the resurrection seriously."[3]

One of five other professional debate judges who evaluated the contestants' argumentation techniques (again Habermas was the victor) felt compelled to write, "I conclude that the historical evidence, though flawed, is strong enough to lead reasonable minds to conclude that Christ did indeed rise from the dead.... Habermas does end up providing 'highly probable evidence' for the historicity of the resurrection 'with no plausible naturalistic evidence against it.' Habermas, therefore, in my opinion, wins the debate."[4]

After earning a doctorate from Michigan State University, where he wrote his dissertation on the resurrection, Habermas received a doctor of divinity degree from Emmanuel College in Oxford, England. He has authored seven books dealing with Jesus rising from the dead, including *The Resurrection of Jesus: A Rational Inquiry; The Resurrection of Jesus: An Apologetic; The Historical Jesus;* and *Did Jesus Rise from the Dead? The Resurrection Debate,* which was based on his debate with Flew. Among his other books are *Dealing with Doubt* and (with J. P. Moreland) *Beyond Death: Exploring the Evidence for Immortality.*

In addition, he coedited *In Defense of Miracles* and contributed to *Jesus under Fire* and *Living Your Faith: Closing the Gap between Mind and Heart.* His one hundred articles have appeared in popular publications (such as the *Saturday Evening Post*), scholarly journals (including *Faith and Philosophy* and *Religious Studies*), and reference books (for example, *The Baker Dictionary of Theology*). He's also the former president of the Evangelical Philosophical Society.

I don't mean to suggest by my earlier description that Habermas is unnecessarily combative; he's friendly and self-effacing in casual conversations. I just wouldn't want to be on the other side of a hockey puck—or an argument—from him. He has an innate radar that helps him zero in on his opponent's vulnerable points. He also has a tender side, which I would discover—quite unexpectedly—before our interview was over.

I found Habermas in his no-nonsense office at Liberty University, where he is currently distinguished professor and chairman of the Department of Philosophy and Theology and director of the master's program in apologetics. The room, with its black file cabinets, metal desk with simulated wood top, threadbare carpet, and folding guest chairs, is certainly no showplace. Like its occupant, it's free from pretension.

"DEAD PEOPLE DON'T DO THAT"

Habermas, sitting behind his desk, rolled up the sleeves of his blue button-down shirt as I turned on my tape recorder and started our interview.

"Isn't it true," I began with prosecutorial bluntness, "that there are absolutely no eyewitnesses to Jesus' resurrection?"

"That's exactly right — there's no descriptive account of the resurrection," Habermas replied in an admission that might surprise people who only have a casual knowledge of the subject.

"When I was young, I was reading a book by C. S. Lewis, who wrote that the New Testament says nothing about the resurrection. I wrote a real big 'No!' in the margin. Then I realized what he was saying: nobody was sitting inside the tomb and saw the body start to vibrate, stand up, take the linen wrappings off, fold them, roll back the stone, wow the guards, and leave."

That, it seemed to me, might pose some problems. "Doesn't this hurt your efforts to establish that the resurrection is a historical event?" I asked.

Habermas pushed back his chair to get more comfortable. "No, this doesn't hurt our case one iota, because science is all about causes and effects. We don't see dinosaurs; we study the fossils. We may not know how a disease originates, but we study its symptoms. Maybe nobody witnesses a crime, but police piece together the evidence after the fact.

"So," he continued, "here's how I look at the evidence for the resurrection: First, did Jesus die on the cross? And second, did he appear later to people? If you can establish those two things, you've made your case, because dead people don't normally do that."

Historians agree there's plenty of evidence that Jesus was crucified, and Dr. Alexander Metherell demonstrated in an earlier chapter that Jesus could not have survived the rigors of that execution. That leaves the second part of the issue: Did Jesus really appear later?

"What evidence is there that people saw him?" I asked.

"I'll start with evidence that virtually all critical scholars will admit," he said, opening the Bible in front of him. "Nobody questions that Paul wrote 1 Corinthians, and we have him affirming in two places that he personally encountered the resurrected Christ. He says in 1 Corinthians 9:1, 'Am I not an apostle? Have I not seen Jesus our Lord?' And he says in 1 Corinthians 15:8, 'Last of all he appeared to me also.'"

I recognized that last quote as being attached to the early church creed that Craig and I had already discussed. As Craig indicated, the first part of the creed (verses 3–4) refers to Jesus' execution, burial, and resurrection.

The final part of the creed (verses 5–8) deals with his post-resurrection appearances: "[Christ] appeared to Peter, and then to the Twelve. After that, he appeared to more than five hundred of the brothers at the same time, most of whom are still living, though some have fallen asleep. Then he appeared to James, then to all the apostles." In the next verse, Paul adds, "And last of all he appeared to me also, as to one abnormally born."

On the face of it, this is incredibly influential testimony that Jesus did appear alive after his death. Here were names of specific individuals and groups of people who saw him, written at a time when people could still check them out if they wanted confirmation. Since I knew that the creed would be pivotal in establishing the resurrection, I decided to subject it to greater scrutiny: Why are historians convinced it's a creed? How trustworthy is it? How far back does it go?

"Do you mind if I cross-examine you on this creed?" I asked Habermas.

He extended his hand as if to invite the inquiry. "Please," he said politely, "go ahead."

"CONVINCE ME IT'S A CREED"

Initially I wanted to determine why Habermas, Craig, and so many other experts are convinced that this passage is a creed of the early church and not just the words of Paul, who wrote the letter to the Corinthian church in which it's contained.

My challenge to Habermas was simple and direct: "Convince me it's a creed."

"Well, I can give you several solid reasons. First, Paul introduces it with the words *received* and *delivered* [or *passed on* in the New International Version], which are technical rabbinic terms indicating he's passing along holy tradition.

"Second," Habermas said, looking down at his hands as he grabbed a finger at a time to emphasize each point he was making, "the text's parallelism and stylized content indicate it's a creed. Third, the original text uses *Cephas* for Peter, which is his Aramaic name. In fact, the Aramaic itself could indicate a very early origin. Fourth, the creed uses several other primitive phrases that Paul would not customarily use, like 'the Twelve,' 'the third day,' 'he was raised,' and others. Fifth, the use of certain words is similar to Aramaic and Mishnaic Hebrew means of narration."

Having run out of fingers, he looked up at me. "Should I go on?" he asked.

"Okay, okay," I said. "You're saying that these facts convince you, as a conservative evangelical Christian, that this is an early creed."

Habermas seemed a bit offended by that admittedly barbed remark. "It's not just conservative Christians who are convinced," he insisted indignantly. "This is an assessment that's shared by a wide range of scholars from across a broad theological spectrum. The eminent scholar Joachim Jeremias refers to this creed as 'the earliest tradition of all,' and Ulrich Wilckens says it 'indubitably goes back to the oldest phase of all in the history of primitive Christianity.'"

That raised the question of how primitive the creed is. "How far back can you date it?" I asked.

"We know that Paul wrote 1 Corinthians between AD 55 and 57. He indicates in 1 Corinthians 15:1–4 that he has already passed on this creed to the church at Corinth, which would mean it must predate his visit there in AD 51. Therefore the creed was being used within twenty years of the resurrection, which is quite early.

"However, I'd agree with the various scholars who trace it back even further, to within two to eight years of the resurrection, or from about AD 32 to 38, when Paul received it in either Damascus or Jerusalem. So this is incredibly early material—primitive, unadorned testimony to the fact that Jesus appeared alive to skeptics like Paul and James, as well as to Peter and the rest of the disciples."

"But," I protested, "it's not really a firsthand account. Paul is providing the list second- or thirdhand. Doesn't that diminish its value as evidence?"

Not to Habermas. "Keep in mind that Paul personally affirms that Jesus appeared to him as well, so this provides firsthand testimony. And Paul didn't just pick up this list from strangers on the street. The leading view is that he got it directly from the eyewitnesses Peter and James themselves, and he took great pains to confirm its accuracy."

That was a strong claim. "How do you know that?" I asked.

"I would concur with the scholars who believe Paul received this material three years after his conversion, when he took a trip to Jerusalem and met with Peter and James. Paul describes that trip in Galatians 1:18–19, where he uses a very interesting Greek word—*historeo*."

I wasn't familiar with the meaning of the word. "Why is that significant?"

"Because this word indicates that he didn't just casually shoot the breeze when he met with them. It shows this was an investigative inquiry. Paul was playing the role of an examiner, someone who was carefully checking this out. So the fact that Paul personally confirmed matters with two eyewitnesses who are specifically mentioned in the creed—Peter and James—gives this extra weight. One of the very few Jewish New Testament scholars, Pinchas Lapide, says the evidence in support of the creed is so strong that it 'may be considered as a statement of eyewitnesses.'"

Before I could jump in, Habermas added, "And later, in 1 Corinthians 15:11, Paul emphasizes that the other apostles agreed in preaching the same gospel, this same message about the resurrection. This means that what the eyewitness Paul is saying is the exact same thing as what the eyewitnesses Peter and James are saying."

I'll admit it: all this sounded pretty convincing. Still, I had some reservations about the creed, and I didn't want Habermas's confident assertions to deter me from probing further.

THE MYSTERY OF THE FIVE HUNDRED

The creed in 1 Corinthians 15 is the only place in ancient literature in which it is claimed that the resurrected Jesus appeared to five hundred people at once. The gospels don't corroborate it. No secular historian mentions it. To me, that raises a yellow flag.

"If this really happened, why doesn't anyone else talk about it?" I asked Habermas. "You'd think the apostles would cite this as evidence wherever they went. As the atheist Michael Martin says, 'One must conclude that it is extremely unlikely that this incident really occurred' and that this therefore 'indirectly casts doubt on Paul as a reliable source.'"[5]

That remark bothered Habermas. "Well, it's just plain silliness to say this casts doubt on Paul," he replied, sounding both astonished and annoyed that someone would make that claim.

"I mean, give me a break! First, even though it's only reported in one source, it just so happens to be the earliest and best-authenticated passage of all! That counts for *something*.

"Second, Paul apparently had some proximity to these people. He says, 'most of whom are still living, though some have fallen asleep.' Paul either knew some of these people or was told by someone who knew them that they were still walking around and willing to be interviewed.

"Now, stop and think about it: you would never include this phrase unless you were absolutely confident that these folks would confirm that they really did see Jesus alive. I mean, Paul was virtually inviting people to check it out for themselves! He wouldn't have said this if he didn't know they'd back him up.

"Third, when you have only one source, you can ask, 'Why aren't there more?' But you can't say, 'This one source is crummy on the grounds that someone else didn't pick up on it.' You can't downgrade this one source that way. So this doesn't cast any doubt on Paul at all—believe me, Martin would love to be able to do that, but he can't do it legitimately.

"This is an example of how some critics want it both ways. Generally, they denigrate the gospel resurrection accounts in favor of Paul, since he is taken to be the chief authority. But on this issue, they're questioning Paul for the sake of texts that they don't trust as much in the first place! What does this say about their methodology?"

I was still having trouble envisioning this appearance by Jesus to such a large crowd. "Where would this encounter with five hundred people have taken place?" I asked.

"Well, the Galilean countryside," Habermas speculated. "If Jesus could feed five thousand, he could preach to five hundred. And Matthew does say Jesus appeared on a hillside; maybe more than just the eleven disciples were there."

Picturing that scene in my mind, I still couldn't help but wonder why someone else didn't report on this event. "Wouldn't it be likely that the historian Josephus would have mentioned something of that magnitude?"

"No, I don't think that's necessarily true. Josephus was writing sixty years later. How long do local stories circulate before they start to die out?" Habermas asked. "So either Josephus didn't know about it, which is possible, or he chose not to mention it, which would make sense because we know Josephus was not a follower of Jesus. You can't expect Josephus to start building the case for him."

When I didn't respond for a moment, Habermas continued. "Look, I'd love to have five sources for this. I don't. But I do have one excellent source—a creed that's so good that German historian Hans von Campenhausen says, 'This account meets all the demands of historical reliability that could possibly be made of such a text.' Besides, you don't need to rely on the reference to the five hundred to make the case for the resurrection. Usually I don't even use it."

Habermas's answer carried some logic. Still, there was another aspect of the creed that weighed on me: it says Jesus appeared first to Peter, whereas John said he appeared first to Mary Magdalene. In fact, the creed doesn't mention any women, even though they're prominently featured in the gospel accounts.

"Don't these contradictions hurt its credibility?" I asked.

"Ah, no," came the reply. "First of all, look at the creed carefully; it doesn't say Jesus appeared *first* to Peter. All it does is put Peter's name first on the list. And since women were not considered competent as witnesses in first-century Jewish culture, it's not surprising that they're not mentioned here. In the first-century scheme of things, their testimony wouldn't carry any weight. So placing Peter first could indicate logical priority rather than temporal priority.

"Again," he concluded, "the creed's credibility remains intact. You've raised some questions, but wouldn't you concede that they don't undermine the persuasive evidence that the creed is early, that it's free from legendary contamination, that it's unambiguous and specific, and that it's ultimately rooted in eyewitness accounts?"

All in all, I was forced to agree that he was right. The weight of the evidence clearly and convincingly supports the creed as being powerful evidence for Jesus' post-resurrection appearances.

So powerful that William Lane Craig, the resurrection expert I interviewed in the previous chapter, said that Wolfhart Pannenberg, perhaps the greatest living systematic theologian in the world, "has rocked modern, skeptical German theology by building his entire theology precisely on the historical evidence for the resurrection of Jesus as supplied in Paul's list of appearances."[6]

Having satisfied myself about the essential reliability of the 1 Corinthians 15 creed, it was time to begin looking at the four gospels, which recount the various appearances by the resurrected Jesus in more detail.

THE TESTIMONY OF THE GOSPELS

I started this line of inquiry by asking Habermas to describe the post-resurrection appearances in Matthew, Mark, Luke, and John.

"There are several different appearances to a lot of different people in the gospels and Acts—some individually, some in groups, sometimes indoors, sometimes outdoors, to softhearted people like John and skeptical people like Thomas," he began.

"At times they touched Jesus or ate with him, with the texts teaching that he was physically present. The appearances occurred over several weeks. And there are good reasons to trust these accounts—for example, they're lacking in many typical mythical tendencies."

"Can you enumerate these appearances for me?"

From memory, Habermas described them one at a time. Jesus appeared

- to Mary Magdalene, in John 20:10–18
- to the other women, in Matthew 28:8–10
- to Cleopas and another disciple on the road to Emmaus, in Luke 24:13–32
- to eleven disciples and others, in Luke 24:33–49
- to ten apostles and others, with Thomas absent, in John 20:19–23
- to Thomas and the other apostles, in John 20:26–30
- to seven apostles, in John 21:1–14
- to the disciples, in Matthew 28:16–20
- And he was with the apostles at the Mount of Olives before his ascension, in Luke 24:50–52 and Acts 1:4–9

"It's particularly interesting," Habermas added, "that C. H. Dodd, the Cambridge University scholar, has carefully analyzed these appearances and concluded that several of them are based on especially early material, including Jesus' encounter with the women, in Matthew 28:8–10; his meeting with the eleven apostles, in which he gave them the Great Commission, in Matthew 28:16–20; and his meeting with the disciples in John 20:19–23, in which he showed them his hands and side."

Again, here was a wealth of sightings of Jesus. This was not merely a fleeting observance of a shadowy figure by one or two people. There were multiple appearances to numerous people, several of the appearances being confirmed in more than one gospel or by the 1 Corinthians 15 creed.

"Is there any further corroboration?" I asked.

"Just look at Acts," replied Habermas, referring to the New Testament book that records the launch of the church. Not only are Jesus' appearances mentioned regularly, but details are provided, and the theme of the disciples being a witness of these things is found in almost every context.

"The key," Habermas said, "is that a number of the accounts in Acts 1–5, 10, and 13 also include some creeds that, like the one in 1 Corinthians 15, report some very early data concerning the death and resurrection of Jesus."

With that Habermas picked up a book and read the conclusion of scholar John Drane:

> The earliest evidence we have for the resurrection almost certainly goes back to the time immediately after the resurrection event is alleged to

have taken place. This is the evidence contained
in the early sermons in the Acts of the Apostles....
[T]here can be no doubt that in the first few chap-
ters of Acts its author has preserved material from
very early sources.[7]

Indeed, Acts is littered with references to Jesus'
appearances. The apostle Peter was especially adamant
about it. He says in Acts 2:32, "God has raised this Jesus
to life, and we are all witnesses of the fact." In Acts 3:15
he repeats, "You killed the author of life, but God raised
him from the dead. We are witnesses of this." He confirms to Cornelius in Acts 10:41 that he and others "ate
and drank with him after he rose from the dead."

Not to be outdone, Paul said in a speech recorded in
Acts 13:31, "For many days he was seen by those who
had traveled with him from Galilee to Jerusalem. They
are now his witnesses to our people."

Asserted Habermas, "The resurrection was undoubtedly the central proclamation of the early church from
the very beginning. The earliest Christians didn't just
endorse Jesus' teachings; they were convinced they had
seen him alive after his crucifixion. *That's* what changed
their lives and started the church. Certainly, since this
was their centermost conviction, they would have made
absolutely sure that it was true."

All of the gospel and Acts evidence—incident after
incident, witness after witness, detail after detail, corroboration on top of corroboration—was extremely impressive.
Although I tried, I couldn't think of any more thoroughly
attested event in ancient history.

There was another question, however, that needed to be raised, this one concerning the gospel that most scholars believe was the first account of Jesus to be written.

MARK'S MISSING CONCLUSION

When I first began investigating the resurrection, I encountered a troubling comment in the margin of my Bible: "The most reliable early manuscripts and other ancient witnesses do not have Mark 16:9–20." In other words, most scholars believe that the gospel of Mark ends at 16:8, with the women discovering the tomb empty but without Jesus having appeared alive to anyone at all. That seemed perplexing.

"Doesn't it bother you that the earliest gospel doesn't even report any post-resurrection appearances?" I asked Habermas.

On the contrary, he didn't seemed disturbed at all. "I don't have a problem with that whatsoever," he said. "Sure, it would be nice if he had included a list of appearances, but here are some things for you to think about:

"Even if Mark does end there, which not everyone believes, you still have him reporting that the tomb is empty, and a young man proclaiming, 'He is risen!' and telling the women that there will be appearances. So you have, first, a proclamation that the resurrection has occurred, and second, a prediction that appearances will follow.

"You can close your favorite novel and say, 'I can't believe the author's not telling me the next episode,' but you can't close the book and say, 'The writer doesn't believe in the next episode.' Mark definitely does. He obviously believed the resurrection had taken place. He ends with the women being told that Jesus will appear in Galilee, and then others later confirm that he did."

According to church tradition, Mark was a companion of the eyewitness Peter. "Isn't it odd," I asked, "that Mark wouldn't mention that Jesus appeared to Peter, if he really had?"

"Mark doesn't mention any appearances, so it wouldn't be peculiar that Peter's isn't listed," he said. "Note, however, that Mark does single out Peter. Mark 16:7 says, 'But go, tell his disciples and Peter, "He is going ahead of you into Galilee. There you will see him, just as he told you."'

"This agrees with 1 Corinthians 15:5, which confirms that Jesus did appear to Peter, and Luke 24:34, another early creed, which says, 'It is true! The Lord has risen and has appeared to Simon,' or Peter.

"So what Mark predicts about Peter is reported to have been fulfilled, in two early and very reliable creeds of the church — as well as by Peter himself in Acts."

ARE THERE ANY ALTERNATIVES?

Without question, the amount of testimony and corroboration of Jesus' post-resurrection appearances is staggering. To put it into perspective, if you were to call each one of the witnesses to a court of law to be cross-examined for just fifteen minutes each, and you went around the clock without a break, it would take you from breakfast on Monday until dinner on Friday to hear them all. After listening to 129 straight hours of eyewitness testimony, who could possibly walk away unconvinced?

Having been a legal affairs journalist who has covered scores of trials, both criminal and civil, I had to agree with the assessment of Sir Edward Clarke, a British High Court judge who conducted a thorough legal analysis of the first Easter: "To me the evidence is conclusive, and over and over again in the High Court I have secured the verdict on evidence not nearly so compelling. As a lawyer I accept the gospel evidence unreservedly as the testimony of truthful men to facts that they were able to substantiate."[8]

But could there be any plausible alternatives that could explain away these encounters with the risen Jesus? Could these accounts be legendary in nature? Or might the witnesses have experienced hallucinations? I decided to raise those issues with Habermas to get his response.

POSSIBILITY 1:
THE APPEARANCES ARE LEGENDARY

If it's true that the gospel of Mark originally ended before any appearances were reported, it could be argued that there's evolutionary development in the gospels: Mark records no appearances, Matthew has some, Luke has more, and John has the most.

"Doesn't that demonstrate that the appearances are merely legends that grew up over time?" I asked.

"For a lot of reasons, no, it doesn't," Habermas assured me. "First, not everybody believes Mark is the earliest gospel. There are scholars, admittedly in the minority, who believe Matthew was written first.

"Second, even if I accept your thesis as true, it only proves that legends grew up over time—it can't explain away the original belief that Jesus was risen from the dead. *Something* happened that prompted the apostles to make the resurrection the central proclamation of the earliest church. Legend can't explain those initial eyewitness accounts. In other words, legend can tell you how a story got bigger; it can't tell you how it originated when the participants are both eyewitnesses and reported the events early.

"Third, you're forgetting that the 1 Corinthians 15 creed predates any of the gospels, and it makes huge claims about the appearances. In fact, the claim involving the biggest number—that he was seen alive by five hundred people at once—goes back to this earliest source! That creates problems for the legendary-development theory. The best reasons for rejecting the legend theory come from the early creedal accounts in 1 Corinthians 15 and Acts, both of which predate the gospel material.

"And fourth, what about the empty tomb? If the resurrection were merely a legend, the tomb would be filled. But it was empty on Easter morning. That demands an additional hypothesis."

POSSIBILITY 2:
THE APPEARANCES WERE HALLUCINATIONS

Maybe the witnesses were sincere in believing they saw Jesus. Perhaps they accurately recorded what took place. But could they have been seeing a hallucination that convinced them they were encountering Jesus when they really weren't?

Habermas smiled at the question. "Do you know Gary Collins?" he asked.

That question took me off guard. Sure, I replied, I know him. "I was in his office just recently to interview him," I said.

"Do you believe he's qualified as a psychologist?" Habermas asked.

"Yes," I answered warily, since I could tell he was setting me up for something. "A doctorate, a professor for twenty years, the author of dozens of books on psychological issues, president of a national association of psychologists—yeah, sure, I'd consider him qualified."

Habermas handed me a piece of paper. "I asked Gary about the possibility that these were hallucinations, and this is his professional opinion," he told me. I looked at the document.

> Hallucinations are individual occurrences. By their very nature only one person can see a given hallucination at a time. They certainly aren't something which can be seen by a group of people. Neither is it possible that one person could somehow induce an hallucination in somebody else. Since an hallucination exists only in this subjective, personal sense, it is obvious that others cannot witness it.[9]

"That," said Habermas, "is a big problem for the hallucination theory, since there are repeated accounts of Jesus appearing to multiple people who reported the same thing.

"And there are several other arguments why hallucinations can't explain away his appearances," he continued. "The disciples were fearful, doubtful, and in despair after the crucifixion, whereas people who hallucinate need a fertile mind of expectancy or anticipation. Peter was hardheaded, for goodness' sake; James was a skeptic—certainly not good candidates for hallucinations.

"Also, hallucinations are comparably rare. They're usually caused by drugs or bodily deprivation. Chances are, you don't know anybody who's ever had a hallucination not caused by one of those two things. Yet we're supposed to believe that over a course of many weeks, people from all sorts of backgrounds, all kinds of temperaments, in various places, all experienced hallucinations? That strains the hypothesis quite a bit, doesn't it?

"Besides, if we establish the gospel accounts as being reliable, how do you account for the disciples eating with Jesus and touching him? How does he walk along with two of them on the road to Emmaus? And what about the empty tomb? If people only thought they saw Jesus, his body would still be in his grave."

Okay, I thought, if it wasn't a hallucination, maybe it was something more subtle.

"Could this have been an example of groupthink, in which people talk each other into seeing something that doesn't exist?" I asked. "As Michael Martin observed, 'A person full of religious zeal may see what he or she wants to see, not what is really there.'"[10]

Habermas laughed. "You know, one of the atheists I debated, Antony Flew, told me he doesn't like it when other atheists use that last argument, because it cuts both ways. As Flew said, 'Christians believe because they want to, but atheists don't believe because they don't want to!'

"Actually, there are several reasons why the disciples couldn't have talked each other into this. As the center of their faith, there was too much at stake; they went to their deaths defending it. Wouldn't some of them rethink the groupthink at a later date and recant or just quietly fall away? And what about James, who didn't believe in Jesus, and Paul, who was a persecutor of Christians—how did they get talked into seeing something? Further, what about the empty tomb?

"And on top of that, this view doesn't account for the forthright language of sight in the 1 Corinthians 15 creed and other passages. The eyewitnesses were at least convinced that they had *seen* Jesus alive, and groupthink doesn't explain this aspect very well."

Habermas paused long enough to pull out a book and cap his argument with a quote from prominent theologian and historian Carl Braaten: "Even the more skeptical historians agree that for primitive Christianity ... the resurrection of Jesus from the dead was a real event in history, the very foundation of faith, and not a mythical idea arising out of the creative imagination of believers."[11]

"Sometimes," concluded Habermas, "people just grasp at straws trying to account for the appearances. But nothing fits all the evidence better than the explanation that Jesus was alive."

"NO RATIONAL DOUBT"

Jesus was killed on the cross—Alexander Metherell has made that graphically clear. His tomb was empty on Easter Morning—William Lane Craig left no doubt about that. His disciples and others saw him, touched him, and ate with him after the resurrection—Gary Habermas has built that case with abundant evidence. As prominent British theologian Michael Green said, "The appearances

of Jesus are as well authenticated as anything in antiq-
uity.... There can be no rational doubt that they occurred,
and that the main reason why Christians became sure of
the resurrection in the earliest days was just this. They
could say with assurance, 'We have seen the Lord.' They
knew it was he."[12]

Before I left Habermas's office, however, I had one
more question. Frankly, I hesitated to ask it, because it
was a bit too predictable and I thought I'd get an answer
that was a little too pat.

The question concerned the importance of the resurrection. I figured if I asked Habermas about that, he'd
give the standard reply about it being at the center of
Christian doctrine, the axis around which the Christian
faith turned. And I was right—he did give a stock answer
like that.

But what surprised me was that this wasn't all
he said. This nuts-and-bolts scholar, this burly and
straight-shooting debater, this combat-ready defender
of the faith, allowed me to peer into his soul as he gave
an answer that grew out of the deepest valley of despair
he had ever walked through.

THE RESURRECTION OF DEBBIE

Habermas rubbed his graying beard. The quick-fire
cadence and debater's edge to his voice were gone. No
more quoting of scholars, no more citing of Scripture, no
more building a case. I had asked about the importance of
the resurrection, and Habermas decided to take a risk by
describing what happened in 1995, when his wife, Deb-

bie, slowly died of stomach cancer. Caught off guard by the tenderness of the moment, all I could do was listen.

"I sat on our porch," he began, looking off to the side at nothing in particular. He sighed deeply, then went on. "My wife was upstairs dying. Except for a few weeks, she was home through it all. It was an awful time. This was the worst thing that could possibly happen."

He turned and looked straight at me. "But do you know what was amazing? My students would call me—not just one but several of them—and say, 'At a time like this, aren't you glad about the resurrection?' As sober as those circumstances were, I had to smile for two reasons. First, my students were trying to cheer me up with my own teaching. And second, it worked.

"As I would sit there, I'd picture Job, who went through all that terrible stuff and asked questions of God, but then God turned the tables and asked *him* a few questions.

"I knew if God were to come to me, I'd ask only one question: 'Lord, why is Debbie up there in bed?' And I think God would respond by asking gently, 'Gary, did I raise my Son from the dead?'

"I'd say, 'Come on, Lord, I've written seven books on that topic! Of course he was raised from the dead. But I want to know about Debbie!'

"I think he'd keep coming back to the same question—'Did I raise my Son from the dead?' 'Did I raise my Son from the dead?'—until I got his point: the resurrection says that if Jesus was raised two thousand years ago, there's an answer to Debbie's death in 1995. And do you know what? It worked for me while I was sitting on the porch, and it still works today.

"It was a horribly emotional time for me, but I couldn't get around the fact that the resurrection *is* the answer for her suffering. I still worried; I still wondered what I'd do raising four kids alone. But there wasn't a time when that truth didn't comfort me.

"Losing my wife was the most painful experience I've ever had to face, but if the resurrection could get me through that, it can get me through anything. It was good for AD 30, it was good for 1995, and it's good beyond that."

Habermas locked eyes with mine. "That's not some sermon," he said quietly. "I believe that with all my heart. If there's a resurrection, there's a heaven. If Jesus was raised, Debbie will be raised. And I will be someday too.

"Then I'll see them both."

DELIBERATIONS
Questions for Reflection or Group Study

1. Habermas reduced the issue of the resurrection down to two questions: Did Jesus die? And was he later seen alive? Based on the evidence you've now seen, how would you answer those questions and why?

2. How influential is the 1 Corinthians 15 creed in your assessment of whether Jesus was seen alive? What are your reasons for concluding that it's significant or insignificant in your investigation?

3. Spend a few minutes to look up some of the gospel appearances cited by Habermas. Do they have the ring of truth to you? How would you evaluate them as evidence for the resurrection?

4. Habermas spoke about how the resurrection had a personal meaning for him. Have you faced a loss in your life? How would belief in the resurrection affect the way you view it?

CONCLUSION

I started my original investigation as a spiritual skeptic, but after having thoroughly investigated the evidence for the resurrection, I was coming to a startlingly unexpected verdict. One final fact—described by a respected philosopher named J. P. Moreland—clinched the case for me.

"When Jesus was crucified," Moreland told me, "his followers were discouraged and depressed. So they dispersed. The Jesus movement was all but stopped in its tracks. Then, after a short period of time, we see them abandoning their occupations, regathering, and committing themselves to spreading a very specific message—that Jesus Christ was the Messiah of God who died on a cross, returned to life, and was seen alive by them.

"And they were willing to spend the rest of their lives proclaiming this, without any payoff from a human point of view. They faced a life of hardship. They often went without food, slept exposed to the elements, were ridiculed, beaten, imprisoned. And finally, most of them were executed in torturous ways. For what? For good intentions? No, because they were convinced beyond a shadow of a doubt that they had seen Jesus Christ alive from the dead."

Yes, people will die for their religious convictions if they sincerely believe they are true. Religious fanatics have done that throughout history. While they may strongly believe in the tenets of their religion, however, they don't know for a fact whether their faith is based on the truth. They simply cannot know for sure. They can only believe.

In stark contrast, the disciples were in the unique position to know for a fact whether Jesus had returned from the dead. They saw him, they touched him, they ate with him. They knew he wasn't a hallucination or a legend. And knowing the truth, they were willing to die for him.

That insight stunned me. The disciples didn't merely *believe* in the resurrection; they *knew* whether it was fact or fiction. Had they known it was a lie, they would never have been willing to sacrifice their lives for it. Nobody willingly dies for something that they know is false. They proclaimed the resurrection to their deaths for one reason alone: they *knew* it was true.

And based on the historical data I had examined, I became convinced they were right. Combined with the other evidence for Jesus that I describe in my book *The Case for Christ*, I concluded that he really is the one and only Son of God, who proved it by rising from the dead.

THE FORMULA OF FAITH

As soon as I reached that monumental verdict, the implications were obvious. If Jesus overcame the grave, he's still alive and available for me to personally encounter. If Jesus conquered death, he can open the door of eternal life for me too. If he has divine power, he has the supernatural ability to guide and transform me as I follow him. As my Creator who has my best interests at heart, he rightfully deserves my allegiance and worship.

Unsure what to do, I turned to a Bible verse I had encountered earlier. John 1:12 says, "Yet to all who received him, to those who believed in his name, he gave the right to become children of God." Essentially, then, the formula for becoming adopted into God's family is:

Believe + Receive = Become.

Because of the evidence, I now *believed* Jesus to be the Son of God. But to become his child, it was necessary for me to *receive* the free gift of forgiveness that he purchased with his life on the cross.

So on November 8, 1981, I talked with God in a heartfelt and unedited prayer, admitting and turning from all of my wrongdoing, and receiving the free gift of forgiveness and eternal life through Jesus. I told him that with his help I wanted to follow him and his ways as best I could from that moment forward.

Some people feel a rush of emotion at such a moment; for me, there was something equally exhilarating: *the rush of reason*.

Looking back, I can see that this was nothing less than the pivotal event of my entire life. Over time my character, values, attitude, priorities, worldview, philosophy, and relationships began to change—for the good.

So much so that a few months after I became a follower of Jesus, our five-year-old daughter, Alison—who had previously only known a father who had been profane, angry, verbally harsh, drunken, and all too often absent—walked up to my wife and said, "Mommy, I want God to do for me what he's done for Daddy."

In effect, she was saying, "If this is what God does to a human being, then that's what I want for me." Even at that early age, she experienced an authentic spiritual transformation that shines through her life to this day.

WHAT'S YOUR VERDICT?

Now, what about you? Maybe this book has helped you come to your own verdict about Jesus, and you're ready to offer the same kind of prayer that changed my life and eternity. Believe me, I'll be cheering you on as you do!

Or maybe you're still a skeptic or seeker. If so, let me challenge you to pursue the truth about Jesus enthusiastically and honestly. Make this a front-burner issue. You might want to whisper a prayer to the God who you're not sure exists, asking him to guide you to the truth about him.

After all, there's a lot riding on your verdict. If Jesus really is the Son of God, then your eternity hinges on how you respond to him. As Jesus said in John 8:24, "If you do not believe that I am the one I claim to be, you will indeed die in your sins."

Those are sober words, offered out of loving concern. In fact, his love for you is so great that he willingly suffered the torture of the cross to pay the penalty for all the wrong things you've ever done. He offers complete forgiveness, his leadership and guidance, and an open door to heaven to all who put their trust in him.

The choice is yours.

FOR FURTHER EVIDENCE

Craig, William Lane. *Reasonable Faith*. Westchester, Ill.: Crossway, 1994.

Geivett, R. Douglas, and Gary R. Habermas, eds. *In Defense of Miracles*. Downers Grove, Ill.: InterVarsity Press, 1997.

Habermas, Gary, and Antony Flew. *Did Jesus Rise from the Dead? The Resurrection Debate*. San Francisco: Harper & Row, 1987.

Habermas, Gary, and J. P. Moreland. *Beyond Death: Exploring the Evidence for Immortality*. Westchester, Ill.: Crossway, 1998.

Hanegraaff, Hank. *The Third Day*. Nashville: W Group, 2003.

Morison, Frank. *Who Moved the Stone?* Grand Rapids: Zondervan, 1987.

Strobel, Lee. *The Case for Christ*. Grand Rapids: Zondervan, 1998.

Wilkins, Michael J. and J. P. Moreland, eds. *Jesus under Fire*. Grand Rapids: Zondervan, 1995.

NOTES

CHAPTER 1: THE MEDICAL EVIDENCE

1. Surah IV: 156–57.

2. Ian Wilson, *Jesus: The Evidence* (1984, reprint, San Francisco: HarperSanFrancisco, 1988*)*, 140.

3. William Lane Craig, *Reasonable Faith* (Westchester, Ill.: Crossway, 1994), 234.

4. D. H. Lawrence, *Love among the Haystacks and Other Stories* (New York: Penguin, 1960), 125.

5. Hugh Schonfield, *The Passover Plot* (New York: Bantam, 1965), 165.

6. Gary Habermas, *The Verdict of History* (Nashville: Nelson, 1988*)*, 56.

7. Michael Baigent, Richard Leigh, and Henry Lincoln, *Holy Blood, Holy Grail* (New York: Delacorte, 1982), 372.

8. Luke Timothy Johnson, *The Real Jesus* (San Francisco: HarperSanFrancisco, 1996), 30.

9. J. W. Hewitt, "The Use of Nails in the Crucifixion," *Harvard Theological Review* 25 (1932), 29–45, cited in Josh McDowell, *The Resurrection Factor* (San Bernardino: Here's Life, 1981), 45.

10. William D. Edwards et al., "On the Physical Death of Jesus Christ," *Journal of the American Medical Association* (March 21, 1986), 1455–63.

CHAPTER 2: THE EVIDENCE OF THE MISSING BODY

1. Gerald O'Collins, *The Easter Jesus* (London: Darton, Longman & Todd, 1973), 134, cited in Craig, *The Son Rises,* 136.

2. For a tape of the debate, see William Lane Craig and Frank Zindler, *Atheism vs. Christianity: Where Does the Evidence Point?* (Grand Rapids: Zondervan, 1993), videocassette.

3. Charles Templeton, *Farewell to God,* (Toronto: McClelland & Stewart, 1996), 120.

4. Michael Martin, *The Case against Christianity* (Philadelphia: Temple University Press, 1991), 78–79.

5. Ibid., 81.

6. Michael Grant, *Jesus: An Historian's Review of the Gospels* (New York: Charles Schribner's Sons, 1977), 176.

7. Apologist Glenn Miller's research of the rabbinical literature supports this. He pointed out: "Rabbi Eleazar ben Azariah, tenth in the descent from Ezra, was very specific: 'A day and a night are an *Onah* ["a portion of time"] and the portion of an *Onah* is as the whole of it'" (J. Talmud, Shabbath 9.3 and b. Talmud, Pesahim 4a).

8. Kirsopp Lake, *The Historical Evidence for the Resurrection of Jesus Christ* (London: Williams & Norgate, 1907), 247–79, cited in William Lane Craig, *Knowing the Truth about the Resurrection* (Ann Arbor, Mich.: Servant, 1988), 35–36.

9. J. N. D. Anderson, *The Evidence for the Resurrection* (Downers Grove, Ill.: InterVarsity Press, 1966), 20.

CHAPTER 3: THE EVIDENCE OF APPEARANCES

1. "Bomb Victim's Body Not in Grave," *Chicago Tribune* (January 14, 1998).

2. Martin, *The Case against Christianity,* 87.

3. Gary Habermas and Antony Flew, *Did Jesus Rise from the Dead? The Resurrection Debate* (San Francisco: Harper & Row, 1987), xiv.

4. Ibid., xv.

5. Martin, *The Case against Christianity,* 90.

6. William Lane Craig, *The Son Rises* (Chicago: Moody Press, 1981), 125.

7. John Drane, *Introducing the New Testament* (San Francisco: Harper & Row, 1986), 99.

8. Michael Green, *Christ Is Risen: So What?* (Kent: Sovereign World, 1995), 34.

9. Also cited in Gary Habermas and J. P. Moreland, *Immortality: The Other Side of Death* (Nashville: Nelson, 1992), 60.

10. Martin, *The Case against Christianity,* 75.

11. Carl Braaten, *History and Hermeneutics,* vol. 2 of *New Directions in Theology Today,* ed. William Hordern (Philadelphia: Westminster Press, 1966), 78, cited in Habermas and Flew, *Did Jesus Rise from the Dead?* 24.

12. Michael Green, *The Empty Cross of Jesus* (Downers Grove, Ill.: InterVarsity Press, 1984), 97, emphasis in original.